PRAISE
for *Becoming TIGERS*

"I am convinced that most Lean Transformations fail due to "a gap" in Leadership, whether it's the front line supervisor, executive, or anywhere in between. Dianne Crampton has done a wonderful job in boiling down the leadership principles and behaviors needed to close this gap and solve this problem with *"Becoming TIGERS – Leading Your Team to Success"*, a quick, helpful read for any current or future leader."

> -Michael Hoseus Former Supervisor, Manager and Executive for Toyota Motor Mfg USA and Co Author of Shingo Award Winning book, *Toyota Culture, The Heart and Soul of the Toyota Way.*

"It was my pleasure to read *"Becoming TIGERS – Leading Your Team to Success"* by Dianne Crampton. Initially I was unsure what to expect as Dianne is a world-class trainer and consultant, and I had not yet read any of her books. Let me begin by saying, I TOTALLY recommend this book for any professional, any parent, and current-or-future-leader, or anyone wishing to enhance their effectiveness as a leader and human being.

"The characters in this story – Derek Alexander, his daughter Raven, and his wife, Martha, provide inspiration and guidance as Derek and Martha work with their daughter on a school assignment. Martha is an important support system, coach, and confidante to Derek. Derek is inspired to follow the examples and learn from the mistakes of the main character, Kali – a frustrated ruler and bully-tyrant towards all for whom he rules and works. This inspirational parable cleverly provides subtle insights into human interaction and group dynamics told through the experiences of two tigers (Kali, Ashoka, and a variety of animals with unique skills and talents).

"I encourage *any* and *all* to read this wonderful story and learn from its valuable lessons. I look forward to using this in my training and consulting work as I build future leaders in the U.S. and abroad."

-Skip Pettit, President of International Training Consortium and CLO Thought Leadership

"First of all, I loved the book. Yes, the book applies to business owners but more importantly to my skills as a parent! After all, a family is very much like a team. I related it to good parenting. Interdependence resonated with me the most. I realized that I have a hard time allowing my kids to "be themselves" and figure things out on how to do things on their own and in their own way.

"I like to hover and direct the "right way" to do things. I loved the Tiger Lord story, but was most drawn to Derek and how he was relating the story back into his own life. The T-graph charts Crampton added are excellent tools for readers to relate back into their own life. When I paused from the book, it kept me thinking… This book certainly is a keeper and something to reread for a lifetime."

-Anna Puchany, Business Owner Head to Heel Massage Therapy

"This is a wonderful book that combines the emotional charm-based learning of an allegory with the substantial content of evidence-based guidance. I continuously noticed my ability to relate the story and its lessons to my own personal and professional experiences. And, despite all the advanced degrees and consulting experience I have, when I set the book down I had created a list of specific actions that I wanted to take to improve my team leadership within the coming weeks. Who among us behaves perfectly in these situations and can't improve with learning (or a reminder of) these fundamental principles?

"I find that reading this story has opened my mind and my heart to much more that I can do to strengthen the people-side of my work. It will be a special gift to everyone fortunate enough to read and learn from it."

-Dr. James Pepitone, co-founder and Director of Technology Transfer for the Humaneering Technology Initiative and HCM 4.0 Innovator

"*Becoming TIGERS – Leading Your Team to Success* by Dianne Crampton approaches the issue of successful teams, with humor and seriousness, in her story within a story latest book. The result is an easy to follow, highly relatable, successful discourse for teams of any size, culture and direction, be they for non-profit or business. The tools Crampton provides helps teams of all types and is quite needed in today's corporate environs where communication is at a standstill most of the time. The parts of the book where Crampton provides simple, clear comparison graphs is most interesting as it shows that the protagonist is clearly capable of making these decisions that can be taken back to his struggling team.

"This book is a perfect resource for not only leadership and management, but also for outside corporate consultants and coaches who are always seeking credible information that can be applied to all types of businesses, from communications to technology. I say get two copies of this book now – one for giving away, the other copy for making notes in the margins!"

> -Joanne Victoria, Life Coach to Leaders & Entrepreneurs and a Life/Work Harmony Specialist, is the author of seven books, including **'Vision with a Capital V – Create the Business of Your Dreams'**. AskJoanneVictoria.com.

"*Becoming TIGERS* by Dianne Crampton is a must-read book for any leader of people to ensure engagement, workplace happiness, AND results. This short but powerful story does what true storytelling is meant to do. It invites me to become a part of someone else's story to create reflection upon my own. With numerous examples, the reader will recall being on one side or the other of each of the trials: Trust, Interdependence, Genuineness, Empathy, Risk, and Success.

"In my work consulting on effectiveness and efficiency for organizations, I have found that team engagement and productivity are of utmost importance and directly tied to profitability. This book provides the lesson in an easy and enjoyable manner that is sure to inspire action."

-Megan Fries, Organizational Strategist and Founder of Frenzy to Freedom

"I really enjoy this book so much!!! What a wonderful book for everyone to benefit from. I enjoyed the dynamic of the father learning from the book with his family and seeing his opportunities as a leader to shift the culture he had instilled and wasn't working. It is great how the book walks through the TIGERS leadership areas and makes it easy to understand and relate to.

"I especially enjoyed the homework reflection areas, making it an ideal resource for teams and growing together by doing a book club. I would recommend everyone read this book and feel confident even the best leaders would be able to see areas to improve, with their own teams."

-Ali Cammelletti, Leadership Coach for Cammelletti Consulting

"Wonderful book! Right from the start, I knew this book was transformational.

As a storyteller myself, I value Dianne's ability and innovative approach to building an authentic team-based work culture. I would highly recommend this for anyone who is tired of the dry management and leadership how-to books out there today.

A good story containing great illustrations from life to inspire business owners and managers. As an attorney, I have litigated many employment law cases and have found that many good intentioned leaders forget the core leadership principals that are prerequisite to being an effective leader. Dianne reinforces the core leadership principles by taking us through is a story that begins with deep, personal exploration, leads to authentic personal growth along the way, and in the end, is all about being of service to others."

-Sejal Thakkar, Lawyer, Trainer, Legal Training Ninja, San Francisco, CA

Becoming TIGERS

Leading Your Team to Success

Three Creeks
Publishing

Three Creeks Publishing
https://www.BecomingTigers.com
© 2019 by Dianne Crampton
All rights reserved.
Printed in the United States of America

ISBN: 978-0-9845082-3-5
Library of Congress Control Number: 2019913954
A CIP catalog record for this book is available from the Library
of Congress.

Special promotions and bulk discounts are available through
Three Creeks Publishing. For details contact the special
marketing department at Intermountain Communications, the
publisher of the Columbia Basin Bulletin at 541-420-0286 or
541-312-8860.

Book design by Angela Guajardo
Cover design by Chris Vacano
Editing by Izabela Zagorski
Internal graphics by Omar Faruk and Rushabh Patel

FIRST EDITION

10 9 8 7 6 5 4 3 2 1

Becoming TIGERS - Leading Your Team to Success
is dedicated to my friend, co-writer, and
book designer Angela Guajardo.
Did Angela make a huge difference in my life?
In more ways than you could count!
Thank you, Angela!

CONTENTS

ACKNOWLEDGEMENTS

I want to express my sincere gratitude for the leaders whose insights and wealth of experience helped me refine *Becoming TIGERS – Leading Your Team to Success*. Thank you for confirming my initial instinct.

In the nearly 30 years that TIGERS has been a viable model for Workgroup and Team Leadership Development, not much in leadership performance has changed. One could actually argue leadership performance is worse now than it was 30 years ago.

This observation started nagging at me in early 2016. We needed a different type of business book—a book that reinforces people in the current and future workforce who value family life and live that life based on a solid family foundation and sense of community.

Ultimately, work must balance family life and an employee's mental and emotional health. To that end, employees require support and training before assuming leadership positions. For me it has become a mantra.

Therefore, we need a different type of story. This is a story that stresses empathy and awareness of what is needed to develop and support all employees.

Thank you Mary McNally, Skip Pettit, James S. Pepitone, Mike Hoseus, Bill Crampton, Angela Guajardo, Izabela Zagorski, Chris Vacano, Joanne Victoria, Ali Cammelletti, Anna Puchany and Megan Fries.

Truly great things happen when people share their insights and helpful suggestions while locking arms to travel in the same direction.

INTRODUCTION

Derek Alexander, this book's protagonist, isn't alone. Many people who excel in their jobs, and want more autonomy and opportunity for advancement, accept leadership positions only to be chewed up and spit out by the organizations they serve. This includes newly assigned project managers lacking leadership and team development skills. It also includes entrepreneurs with good business ideas who find themselves hit with high team turnover. These folks, no matter how hard they work, never really get off the ground.

I grew up in an era where the sports television show, *Wild World of Sports*, showed a downhill slalom skier at peak speed catching an edge, hurling, bouncing and sliding down the hill upside down, right side up and every which way, while poles, skies, hat and gloves flew in different directions. The skier didn't move much after that fall. The announcer called it the agony of defeat.

Perhaps it feels that way for so many well-meaning leaders

who experience their leadership failure – the agony of defeat – in a public and personal way.

Perhaps you are one of these leaders. If not, perhaps you know a manager or business owner who is feeling defeated.

Since our last book, *TIGERS Among Us – Winning Business Team Cultures and Why They Thrive*, was published ten years ago, not much has changed for emerging leaders. In fact, not much has changed since the *TIGERS Model for Group and Leadership Development* first emerged in the late 1980s and early 1990s.

In *TIGERS Among Us* we gave readers the research and the breakdown of the 6 TIGERS Principles. We also demonstrated how four different leaders with businesses of 10 to 1,800 employees wove the 6 TIGERS principles of trust, interdependence, genuineness, empathy, risk resolution and success into their operations.

The current book before you tells the story of a manager you might very well know who must improve his leadership skills in order to save his job. With the help of a loving and supportive family and a weekend school project for his daughter, Raven, Derek Alexander is split between family and the anxiety of what he needs to produce by Monday afternoon to save his job.

Derek's boss confronted him on Friday afternoon with an important written performance review. While performing exit interviews with employees who left the team and company, Derek's boss discovers that at least one employee quit because of Derek.

"He is a terrible manager," the employee reports and goes into some detail why.

There are many good leadership books that give you an itemized list of what to do to improve your skills. Along the story theme of Who Moved My Cheese, in *Becoming TIGERS – Leading Your Team to Success*, we focus on leadership through a parable.

We believe stories, such as the one this book tells, are the best way to share a problem and explore actions that can be taken to improve the situation.

Why do the issues considered in this book matter? Excellent leaders can inspire loyalty. They can create belonging and inclusion. They can demand excellence. On the other hand, poisonous work environments can cripple organizations.

In a recent study produced by the Society for Human Resource Management, toxic work cultures damage morale, injure productivity and erode bottom lines. For example, employee turnover caused by toxic culture cost employers more than $223 billion over the past five years.

That is lost revenue that did not end up in the pockets of employees, in new innovation or in their communities. It is lose-lose all the way around.

Ultimately, it is poor management that leads to poor culture. And, managers can only perform as well as they have been trained. It is now time to break this cycle for a couple of reasons.

First, leadership development is still a challenge. It takes time and often time away from the workplace to train leaders. Yet many executives continue the sink or swim approach to leadership advancement and still select people because they get things done and not because they have demonstrated the ability to lead.

Leaders in the 21st Century must do both. They must get things accomplished through employees who they coach, train and develop. At the same time, they must improve their own skills – even during times of change.

Second, too many managers now feel overwhelmed, confused and stressed. The rules they grew up with are changing. They realize it is nearly impossible to improve from a shaky foundation, and they don't know where to start.

As you will see, the parable provided to Derek through his daughter's weekend reading project ignites his imagination. He examines his own behavior and identifies ways to improve his shaky foundation to become an effective leader.

"Yesterday I was clever, so I wanted to change the world.
Today I am wise, so I am changing myself."
Rumi

CHAPTER 1
The Wakeup Call

Derek Alexander entered his home with his back hunched, tie loosened and short hair sticking up from running his hands through it a million times during his shift. The sight of his nine-year-old daughter, Raven, looking up over a book from the dining table lifted the weight of his rough day. However, the tense heaviness settled right back down as he switched from his shoes to his cozy loafers because Derek was worried. Something soft and comfortable wrapping his feet brought some relief, but it didn't change how bad his day had been.

And he had to go back in on Monday. He internally winced before mustering the energy to plant a kiss on his daughter's forehead.

"Hi, Daddy," Raven said. "You look sad. I drew this for you." She handed him a piece of paper with a detailed drawing only a parent would be proud of, but the gesture warmed his heart all the same.

Derek sank into the chair beside her and studied the color pencil drawing of a tiger leading several animals over a bridge. The tiger held its head high like it was roaring. Behind the tiger followed a big gray blob with the telltale lines of a trunk and tusks that meant it was supposed to be an elephant. There was also a monkey, and what looked like a gray bear, and some birds in the scribbly blue sky. He smiled. "This is wonderful! Thank you, Raven. What inspired you to draw this?"

"It's from a really good book at school that we just finished reading this week." She lifted a few pages of vocabulary homework to reveal a children's book depicting an oil painting of a tiger on the cover.

The tiger's intense gaze drew Derek in and for a moment he felt like the creature observed him like it was studying him, but Raven moved the book, breaking the spell. He blinked and saw the book cover for what it was — a painting.

"It's called *The Tiger Lord's Trials*. It's a story about the power of teamwork. We are learning about teamwork in Mrs. Walter's class right now. It is supposed to help us when we work on school projects. You and mom get to read it with me over the weekend!"

A grimace formed on his face before he could stop himself.

"You have to!" exclaimed Raven as disappointment flashed accusingly through her eyes.

All he wanted to do was eat dinner and go to bed. He had no energy left.

Derek's wife, Martha, walked into the room and gently placed her hands on his shoulders, giving him a reassuring squeeze. "I'll read it to you, sweetie."

His wife and daughter were the best things that ever happened to him. They were the motivation that drove him to get up and face the work day. Without them, he would have quit his job a long time ago and found another place with better employees to manage.

"But what about Daddy?" Raven pouted, fixing Derek with an adorable pleading gaze.

"Daddy's had a long day at work. He's going to need his rest. I'll make sure to read it to you tonight."

Raven looked sadly at the book and her homework. "Daddy's always having long days at work."

"I'm sorry, Raven," Derek said. "We have this really big project that needs to get done. We're behind and it's just not going well."

"Why?"

The chaos of missed deadlines, subpar work, lots of reprimanding and one of his employees quitting swirled in his thoughts. How could he possibly explain the nightmare in the office to a nine-year-old? And then that talk with his boss, Amity...

"I wouldn't mind hearing, too," Martha said, returning to the stove, pulling Derek;s attention back to his family. "You've been so stressed lately. I wish I knew how to help."

The delightful smell of homemade pasta sauce and fresh-made meatballs made Derek's stomach growl. Lunch had been so long ago. Had he even eaten lunch? He couldn't remember. His days blended together. He often worked through breaks and meals. Today, all he could remember was Amity's ultimatum. He had until Monday to come up with a plan on how to fix the problems at work, and he definitely didn't have time for his daughter's homework.

Derek's lower back spasmed and he grit his teeth as he tried to massage out the aching knot. He was only in his mid thirties. He wasn't supposed to be having back problems like this. Thankfully, a bit of kneading coaxed the knot to relax and the pain ebbed, allowing him some time to think. "There's nothing you can do, other than keep on being a wonderful wife," he said. "What I need are more competent employees that know how to do their job. I had to fire one person and another one quit. We're behind enough as it is."

"Sounds like you need clones of yourself," Martha said as she placed a steaming plate of spaghetti and three large meatballs in front of Derek.

"That would be wonderful," Derek said, and then murmured thanks for the food. Clones *would* fix the problem. If only it were a viable option.

"What's clones?" Raven said.

"A clone is..." Derek said and went on to explain them to her.

Her eyes widened. "So I could have two daddies? One that goes to work and another one to read and play with me?"

He laughed. Raven's sweet innocence was such a breath of relief from the day's craziness. "That would be nice!" Derek turned to his wife. "We keep hiring people that seem so promising. They interview well and everything but after only a couple of months, they turn out not to be as good as we'd expected. We're burning through employees. Hardly any of them last one year. It's hurting everyone's morale, including mine. And then—" He cut himself off, unable to speak the truth.

Derek, John said in his exit interview that he left because of you. He said you're a terrible boss. With all this turnover tied to you and your team, I'm inclined to believe there's truth to his statement.

Shutting his eyes, Derek grimaced as dread roiled around in his chest. Those words had blindsided him. How could he be the reason for all this madness?

A gentle hand touched his arm.

"Let's talk after we eat." Martha's pale eyes were full of concern, yet brimming with love. She set down food for herself and their daughter. Together, they filled up on a meal complete with a covered basket of garlic bread in the middle of the table. He ate some pasta and chopped up a meatball. With every bite a little tension in his back eased. The sauce was smooth and delectable, the meatballs perfectly cooked and seasoned, and the noodles went down smoothly.

"This is wonderful, Martha. Thank you. Maybe I should hire you."

She laughed. "And then who would run my website business?"

Martha had started up her own business two years ago when Raven entered the first grade. It was doing so well that she now had a thriving home office and a team of developers that shared a co-working place at a local business incubator. She loved her job and employees loved working with her. It was an ideal workplace environment. Why couldn't Derek experience the same at his own workplace? "Okay, okay," he said with a small smile. "You win."

Raven chatted away between bites as Derek and Martha listened in silence, offering up the occasional response to keep their daughter smiling and reminding her to keep eating. She went on a bit about the tiger book and teamwork before jumping to something about recess, a bully who was taken to the principal's office, and then their trip to the library and so on. Derek's plate was empty and his stomach full by the time Raven switched to talking about monkeys.

They washed the dishes as a family, Derek scrubbing everything down, Martha toweling them dry, and Raven—with the help of standing on a chair—returning plates and cups to the hanging cupboards. Derek normally found washing dishes cathartic. Today, he couldn't stop thinking about everything written down in John's exit interview, and Amity's ultimatum to turn himself and his workplace around. The only thing saving him from giving in to despair was the thought that the company hadn't simply fired him.

With the last of the silverware safely tucked away in the drawer, and Raven preoccupied with her vocabulary homework in the adjacent living room, Martha said, "So, do you have any idea what's causing such high turnover? That's usually a sign that something's wrong."

"I thought I did," Derek said and his chest tightened. "I thought my employees were simply not good enough for the job. I keep trying to whip them into shape but none of them seem to be able to learn and much less care." He took a seat at the dinner table and ran his fingertips along the tiger book's cover. "The person who quit had an exit interview with my boss."

"And not with you?" Martha pressed a button on the Keurig machine and popped a K-cup in the dispenser. "That seems strange."

"Not after what he said in the interview," Derek sighed.

Martha furrowed her brows. She slowly took a seat next to him, wringing the dish towel.

Derek took a deep breath. "He quit because of me," he said in a small voice. "Not because of the job... because of me. Amity had caught him before he could leave the building, and he unloaded all his frustrations in a long rant. He even put a few statements in writing." Derek retrieved his photocopied version of the statement and tossed it on the table. "Amity spoke with other employees one on one and they all expressed the same frustration. Other people want to quit but don't have other jobs to go to yet. It's not the job that's making them want to leave; it's me. I don't get what I'm doing wrong."

Martha read through the statement, her face creasing with greater concern as she reached the bottom of the page. "Do you believe them?" she said calmly, her boss voice, a voice she sometimes used on Derek when he got too verbally forceful.

"I ran some numbers. I'm the project manager with the highest turnover in the entire company." He leaned back in his chair, staring at the ceiling and the swirls that had been stroked into the white paint. "The person behind me has a fifth of the rate I do. I cost the company a good ten grand per lost employee. The hiring process, training new employees, lost labor, and so on, are eroding company profit."

Martha set the paper down and flattened it against the lacquered wood of the table. "Those are pretty telling numbers."

Derek nodded, unable to look away from the ceiling. "I have until Monday morning to come up with an action plan on how to improve my performance." Amity hadn't said what the alternative was if Derek failed to deliver, but he didn't need much imagination to know he'd be emptying his office of his personal belongings.

"Read the tiger book with us," Martha said.

Derek peeled his gaze from the ceiling. "Are you really sure that's how I should be spending my time this weekend?"

"Yes," she said with a nod. "They did their first read through this week and her homework is to reread it with us and have us discuss it. It's a children's book. It won't take long to read, and it has a brilliant message I believe you'll find useful."

"You think a children's book is going to save my job?" It was more a statement than a question.

"I think the lessons it teaches will save your job."

"This is ridiculous!" Derek threw his hands up in exasperation. Their daughter curiously looked up at them from the living room floor. He waved to her and told her to go back to playing.

Martha leaned closer. "Honey, I wouldn't suggest it if I didn't think it would help you. I already read it earlier this week in case Raven had any questions. The content is directly applicable to your work situation."

Derek let out a long breath. His wife was trying to help him. He took another one and remained quiet until he was calm enough to wholly believe what his wife was encouraging. Martha wasn't his enemy in this. "What are the lessons?" Derek asked softly.

"Read the book with us and find out," she replied with a smile.

***

Come their daughter's bedtime, Derek found himself seated on one side of Raven's bed, Martha on the other, a family sandwich wrapped under a comforter with unicorns and stars on it. He still didn't believe this was what he needed to do right now, but at least it made his wife and daughter happy.

Gosh, it had been so long since he'd last read to Raven. She wiggled so she lay with her head propped up on her pillow, blanket pulled up under her chin, and big eyes fixed on the book's cover.

Derek angled the matching unicorn bedside lamp so he could better see the book. Once again, the tiger's intense gaze stared back at him as if it were alive. He ran his fingers down the cover, admiring the artwork and the feel of a book in his hands. It had been too long for sure. He opened the book and the smell of paper and ink filled his nose—not the smell of a giant printer spitting out pages nonstop, but the smell of paper carefully bound and stamped with thousands upon thousands of little black letters that formed a story. He breathed deeply as he turned to the title page.

"*The Tiger Lord's Trials*," Derek said in his story voice and looked at his daughter, who was already enraptured and wiggling her feet in anticipation. "A tale about the power of teamwork and how to lead teams." Teamwork. That was something the exit interview had made painfully obvious was lacking from him and his team. Derek flipped to the next page, the first chapter, that was complete with illustrations.

CHAPTER 2
The Mudslide

Once upon a time, there were two great animal tribes led by two great tiger lords. They were brothers, who lived deep in the jungles of India surrounded by trees so tall they looked like they touched the sky. The ground was always wet and soft with fallen leaves, and covered in bushes big enough to hide elephants. Scattered among the trees and bushes were moss-covered, broken buildings left behind by humans many years ago.

The air perpetually smelled of rain and earth. It was the smell of home. During the day, birdsong and monkey calls filled the air. At night, all was quiet except for wind whispering through the leaves and hanging vines.

The two great tiger lords were named Kali and Ashoka, and they were as opposite as day and night. Ashoka was revered and loved by his tribe. He took care of every last animal under his care no matter how big or how small—from the elephants to the frogs and everything in between. Everyone was important and they each knew that. Everyone did their job and did it well, and, as a result, everyone prospered.

Kali, on the other hand, was feared by his tribe. He took care of his animals, big and small, too, but only because it was necessary as lord of the tribe. Everyone had an important job to do, from gathering food and building shelters, to protecting their territory and alerting the others of intruders. No one went hungry, but no one seemed happy, not even the tiger lord, himself.

Both tribes worked towards the same goal but, like their tiger lords, the results were as opposite as could be. Ashoka's tribe seemed to always have more food, bigger and sturdier homes, and happier animals. Their village was full of sturdy, wooden homes, nests in the canopy and in the healthy vines. It looked like a paradise from Kali's side of the river. Everyone in Ashoka's tribe spent a lot of time together and they looked genuinely happy.

The only thing Kali's tribe had were unhappy animals. He had fewer tribe members, less food to go around, and a village full of homes in need of repairs. The animals living in the trees hid when they weren't working. The animals that lived on the ground disappeared in their homes, too. Everyone kept to themselves. Half the time, it looked like hardly anyone lived there.

Every day, the morning creatures from both tribes rose with the sun to either gather food scattered among the vibrant trees and shrubs, patrol their respective side of the river, fish for mahseer (which were quite tasty), or graze for a morning meal in the nearby fields. Some even carried water back to the villages so the young and old could quench their thirst with ease and minimal danger.

Some days the river swelled and rushed by as if it were angry, but the animals knew it had simply rained upriver. Most days the river was a moving mirror to the sky above, but, unlike the sky, danger lay below. This included crocodiles and pythons, creatures that preferred to live tribeless. Bringing water back into the villages protected more of the defenseless animals from becoming a meal.

Kali's tribe never seemed to have enough water for the young and old. They always ran out shortly after the sun went down and he would have to force the sloth bears and water buffalo to gather more. Usually, it took no more than stern words, a few roars and a flash of his large fangs as he hissed to get his tribe members moving.

They'd complain about the crocodiles and pythons but Kali accompanied them, watching their every move and the river, too. He would jump in and attack if anything threatened his tribe, but it was up to the sloth bears and water buffalo to do their job and fetch water. It wasn't Kali's fault that they hadn't fetched enough during the day.

Still, no matter how much he roared or growled, no matter how closely he watched them gather water, the tribe kept running out a little faster each week. For the life of him, Kali couldn't figure out why...until he noticed a trail of water droplets following the water buffalo. Water was dripping from their buckets. A few more stern words and some gibbons quickly made new buckets out of vines and thatch. This stopped the running out of water problem, but only barely.

Ashoka's tribe never ran out of water. In fact, it was so plentiful that his water buffalo had offered Kali's tribe extra water buckets hanging from their curved horns several times. Each time, Kali sent them away without taking a single drop. His animals would never learn to do their jobs correctly or well if someone else did it for them. His animals did not deserve any help.

Water was not the only problem. The hunters and gatherers took longer and longer to bring back food. Even the fishing birds and beasts caught fewer fish. Kali drove them to work harder, hunt and gather for longer hours, but the results were never satisfactory. Every so often, a leopard or a bear would head out into the jungle and never come back. Other animals, especially the birds, would leave Kali's tribe for Ashoka's. This infuriated him to no end.

The other day he completely lost his temper when a crested hawk-eagle family abandoned his tribe for Ashoka's. Kali pursued them on land while the family flew across the river until he splashed to a halt on the muddy bank, roaring, "Get back here now! You belong to my tribe. I did not give you permission to leave."

But the hawks flew onward as if they hadn't heard, the parents flapping occasionally to remain aloft as their young flew ahead. Kali growled and swatted at the river, spraying water everywhere. He took a deep breath. "You will not be welcome if you ever decide to come back! I hereby cast you out. You are no longer a part of my tribe."

The hawks sailed well out of hearing without faltering. Perhaps they hadn't heard. The river was wide again and rushing along with the occasional branch bobbing by. The sky was perfectly clear overhead, but branches floating downriver meant there had been a storm elsewhere.

Kali turned around and was met with the sight of his tribe staring at him. Frogs, elephants, cobras, buffalo, macaques, leopards and even a pair of sloth bears watched as if afraid to move. And afraid they should be. They were all incompetent, not one of them trustworthy. He flattened his ears. "Get back to work. The sun will start going down soon. And we had better not run out of water or food tonight!"

The cobras slithered off, disappearing into the tall grass. Colorful frogs hopped onto the elephants' tusks to be willingly carried away. The leopards and sloth bears lowered their heads before padding back into the village. All of the downtrodden animals hurried back to work. Kali allowed himself a smug smile at the sight of them obeying his orders.

That night, water shortage wasn't a problem, and it wasn't because the sloth bears and water buffalo had done their jobs well, for once.

Frequent lightning and thunder preceded heavy clouds rolling in, blotting out the stars and moon. When the rains came, they came hard and fast. Kali took it upon himself to make sure his entire village had taken shelter and growled at anyone who was foolish enough to try and leave their homes.

"But Lord Kali, our roof is leaking," the father of a civet family said. All of them had damp spotted fur. "We need to move to a dryer place."

Kali was already soaked nose to tail tip and didn't care about a leaky roof. Water dripped off his whiskers. "Then you should have made sure the macaques, gibbons and elephants had repaired your home. If, once the rains stop, I find out that you have left your home, I will kick you out of my tribe. Stay put if you know what's good for you."

The father civet's round eyes widened, but he lowered his head in obedience. "Yes, Lord Kali." He nudged the wood door with his shoulder. It closed with a satisfying thunk. Kali nodded in satisfaction and continued his patrol.

As the night progressed, the rains worsened. Kali enlisted a few leopards, sloth bears and elephants to help him dig families out of homes that had crumbled. The winds blew in nearly sideways, hissing and howling through the leaves as it bent the trees over. Kali ended up having to house the civet family with their neighbors, but at least no one was hurt and they'd listened to him. Later, he was going to have to have a few critical words with his builders about the state of disrepair. Homes wouldn't be crumbling if they'd simply done their jobs correctly.

It wasn't until Kali and his helpers moved an Indian tree-shrew family out of the trees and into a honey badger's home that he realized the water was rising under his paws. Each step sloshed in several inches of muddy water, and each lightning flash showed a village that looked like it had been engulfed by the river itself.

Kali ordered his leopards, sloth bears and elephants to carry on without him. "I need to check on the river." He galloped off.

The trek across the village was long and wet. Despite their inferiority to Ashoka's tribe, they were still one of the largest tribes in India's jungles. The rows of homes, laid out in a circular pattern, seemed long and endless. The closer Kali drew to the riverbank, the deeper the water got. By the time he reached the edge of the village, the water had risen to his belly. Clumps of leaves and tiny branches hit his legs with every step, reducing him to a walk. The flowing water further slowed him with its constant pressure, but he plodded forward until he realized he couldn't tell where the river ended and the shore began. Lightning flashed, making it bright as day for a moment. There was nothing but water in every direction. He couldn't even see any tall grass sticking out.

A wave of fear passed through him as the jagged back of a crocodile slipped under the water's surface, its movements erased by the rainfall. It would have made his hackles rise if he weren't soaked through. Kali took a step backward, at a loss for what to do.

Another flash of lightning allowed him to capture a quick glimpse of Ashoka's village. A procession of every last animal moved in a mass exodus towards higher ground farther downriver. The villages were nestled at the base of a mountain, split by a river that poured into a ravine that opened up opposite the mountain. The largest and strongest animals oversaw the procession.

The sight filled Kali with rage. How could they abandon their homes so easily? This was just a storm. Both tribes had weathered many of them over the past several years. There was no reason to treat this storm any differently.

His rage gave him a plan and his paws carried him back to

the village.

Kali's resolve faltered at the sight of almost every home topped with their respective families huddled on thatch roofs. The village was flooded and a few homes had been washed away. Elephants, water buffalo and rhinoceroses had gathered smaller animals onto their backs, but there wasn't much room left.

Despite the sight of so much water and ruin, Kali wasn't going to let them abandon the village so easily. Crocodiles couldn't hunt in this weather. He was going to show Ashoka's tribe how much braver and more determined Kali's tribe was. They would not leave just because of some minor flooding.

Kali plodded over to the nearest elephants and opened his mouth, but a flock of several species of birds, led by crested hawk-eagles, darted out of the swaying trees, their screeches making Kali wince.

"Mudslide! Run!" the eagles cried in voices that pierced the wind. "A great mudslide is headed this way. Flee the village!" The other birds screeched in agreement and alarm.

At first, Kali thought it was a lie. This was just a trick to make them leave. They all clearly wanted out. But he felt it in his paw pads, a small vibration in the sodden ground that even the mud between his toes could not hide. The truth sank in and rose to his throat. He let out a roar to signal his tribe to flee the village. Flooding was one thing. A mudslide would bury them alive if they didn't get to higher ground.

"Flee the village!" Kali shouted. "Get to higher ground. All large animals carry as many as you can." He darted among elephant legs and stomping water buffalos, wrenching open door after door with a swipe of his powerful paws, and yelled at anyone left inside to flee.

One macaque family was so terrified that all five of them latched onto his sodden back the moment the door flew open, and wouldn't let go no matter how much he growled at them. However, the vibrations under his paws were growing, so he galloped off to the next home and little fingers continued to pull his fur, holding on for dear life.

The next home contained mice that scurried down from the top of the door frame and hopped onto tiger and macaque alike, beady eyes wide with terror. The home after that spilled forth a trio of sodden, yellow martens that also climbed on before he could growl at them to swim instead.

Initially, Kali thought he was hearing the crackling of a nearby lightning strike, but when it continued to crackle, instead of turning to rumbling, he glanced at the mountain. A lightning flash showed dozens upon dozens of trees snapping and falling over. Mud, rocks and fallen trees spilled their way through the gaps, bounding over and around obstacles like a writhing ball of snakes.

The mudslide was here! Kali roared one more time and his tribe fled the village. "This way!" He doubled back to redirect panicking buffalo and bulls to follow the elephants who were carving a path through the deepening water. He had to gnash his fangs at a few to stop them from running right at the mudslide. One bucked at him, but, thankfully, the hooves swung wide.

Soon, the terrified animals escaped the village. In addition to his other frightened passengers, Kali found himself burdened with flying squirrels. As he guided his tribe out of the village, he found he could move no faster than a trot under their combined weight. Other animals swam towards him but he carefully scooped them up with his teeth and tossed them onto buffalo and blue bulls, their little legs flailing until they landed on heaving flanks.

The cracking of toppling trees grew so loud that he could no longer hear the rain. The mudslide poured between the trees lining the outskirts of his village. Trees fell, the ground shook harder, and his tribe began running faster than before. Kali abandoned his efforts to oversee his tribe's movements and found the strength to run for the head of the procession. They all had to flee, even him. Whoever got buried in mud…well, it was just too bad for them if they didn't move fast enough. He had placed himself in danger for as long as he could.

The cracking turned into a rumbling roar as the mudslide engulfed their village. Kali and the tribe hustled up a grassy hillside dotted with shrubs. The hillside arced and rolled towards the mountain, but it also curved around the village in a wide sweep. Kali ran part way up the hill and shook off the animals clinging to his back. All but one macaque let go. Kali growled at the sodden creature, but its eyes were glazed over in shock. "Get him off me, now," Kali said to the other macaques. Little hands and arms reached for their companion and tugged as one. He roared in pain as their small fingers ripped at his fur, causing all but the clinging monkey to cower. He ordered them back to the task. They tentatively reached for him and he growled. "Get him off! Now."

It took a bit of prying and biting back more angry roars, but the last macaque finally let go. Kali shook his flanks, spraying water everywhere, and bounded down the hill just in time to watch the mudslide swallow the village.

Pieces of branches, trunks and homes roiled in the flowing mud and water, devouring everything in its path. Heavy thunks and the crack of snapping wood mingled with the downpour and intermittent thunder. Elephants trumpeted, beasts let out roars of alarm, gibbons howled, and monkeys let out ear-splitting keels. However, the last of his tribe was still approaching the base of the hill. They weren't going to make it.

Kali sped his way to the back of the procession as more homes folded under the unstoppable tide of the mudslide. The stragglers turned at the sound of snapping wood and Kali roared, hoping they would take it as a command to keep moving. There were dozens of animals in the mudslide's path. He couldn't save them all from their own slowness.

The smaller animals, riding atop the rhinos bringing up

the rear, must have sensed the danger. They scurried from back to back along the larger animals and hurried onto the hillside, turning around only once until they knew they were safe. They urged the rhinos, water buffalo and the rest in their tiny voices to hurry.

Kali sped past them and around the rhinos, and stood behind them. "Move faster, you fools! Get up the hill. Now!" He charged into one armored hide, ramming it with his shoulder. The beast lurched forward and bumped into a water buffalo with its massive, pointed horn. The buffalo let out a deep bleat and started running. The other four buffalo sensed their herd member's sudden rise in stress and took off with him, their rumbling hooves blending with the mudslide's deep, earthy rumble.

The rhinos had yet to pick up the pace, including the one he'd shoved. Kali ran up beside them. "Run, you fools!" The giant beasts continued to plod forward, mouths agape and foaming, their big black eyes glazed with fatigue. They didn't even blink when rain hit them. Despite their great hearing, the nearest one didn't know his tiger lord trotted alongside him. "I said run!" Kali snarled.

Again, no response.

Growling, Kali returned to the nearest one's flanks and clawed at him—not enough to draw blood, but enough that the beast would feel it through his thick hide. The rhino grunted and finally moved faster with bounding strides, revealing a calf that had been wedged between its parents.

More and more sticks whipped through the water, and faster, too. The water level was rising. Kali stumbled his way over to the other parent, got it moving with a claw-filled prod, and then turned to the calf that was half as big as him. It was panting just as hard as his parents. Kali was gasping for breath as well, but his work wasn't done.

Diving underwater, he squeezed under the calf and

straightened his legs. It was like trying to lift the weight of the world. The river tried to push them sideways, but his limbs finally straightened. His legs trembled as they got pummeled by debris. He rose triumphantly, the calf on his back, and shook the muddy water from his head.

Gibbons and sloth bears stretched their arms and an elephant reached with her trunk as Kali half carried, half dragged the calf to safety. Each step was a battle to keep both his footing and their heads above water, but thankfully the calf didn't struggle or panic. It just kicked its legs like it was trying to swim, attempting to guide them closer to safety. Bigger branches collided with them as they neared, and the water rose to where he could barely touch the ground. They began drifting sideways as the river took them. The animals on shore moved with them.

"Take... the calf," Kali said between breaths. He hauled them both over a tree trunk and splashed back into the water, becoming completely submerged for a heartbeat before he broke the surface again and gulped in air. "Hurry." He panted. He didn't have the energy to yell. The calf was so heavy and the water so deep that his front paws no longer found the bottom. He propelled them forward on his hind legs as he paddled with his front paws.

Long-clawed, paws brushed the calf's stumpy horn but couldn't hold. An elephant trunk loomed over both calf and tiger but the calf's body lurched as the elephant lost hold, too. Kali took a deep breath and heaved them both forward as a wall of mud and branches swiftly approached.

The gibbons and sloth bears cried out in triumph as they finally hauled the calf out of the water and onto the hill. Kali reached out for the trunk extended towards him but it was the last thing he saw before the mudslide dragged him under.

CHAPTER 3
The Cost of Poor Leadership

It was quiet. So nice and quiet, yet so terribly painful. Eyes still closed, Kali groaned, and then took a deep breath. He hurt all over, especially his right side. He heaved a great sigh and licked his lips. Thirsty. His mouth was parched and he was in so much pain. He opened one eye, and then the other.

It was light out, the twilight of predawn. The storm was long gone, given way to stars and the sliver of a pale yellow horizon. Kali lifted his head and winced as pain lanced down his neck.

"He's awake!"

Kali gingerly turned his head at the voice. One of the gibbons, Rekhan, lumbered over to him and the tiger lord let out a warning growl, stopping the gibbon so fast that it slipped on the grass. A pair of leopards stepped between Kali and Rekhan.

The tiger lord tried to rise but fire filled his legs and he collapsed back onto the ground. He bared his fangs and tried to focus on the gibbon as panic filled him. He couldn't stand.

"Where's the rest of the tribe?"

"Farther up the hill," Rekhan said, his hairy face lined with concern. "The mudslide chased us a little more before it was all over."

Kali gingerly turned his head but it hurt all the same. Sure enough, he recognized the backs of his beasts huddled together at the edge of the jungle, each of them lined with a hint of silvery light in the almost utter darkness.

"The village is gone," Rekhan said sadly. "There is nothing but mud and ruin, but it appears everyone survived. We thought we'd lost you."

Kali could barely recall pushing the rhino calf to safety before the darkness took over. There had been a rush of movement, jostling, and slamming into things while fully submerged, and then he'd woken here, in thick grass, barely able to move. He tried to rise again but could only manage to pivot enough to see where the village should have been.

In its place lay a hunk of mud with a roiling river cutting through another great slab of mud. Ashoka's tribe was nowhere to be seen. The thatched village was gone, covered in mud, and many broken trees littered the now engulfed village.

Kali assessed the situation and then made a decision. "Wake the tribe. Send some to gather food. Order the rest to start digging out the village. It's not gone. It's buried."

Rekhan glanced at the muddy ruins and his eyes filled with incredulous despair as he turned back to his lord once more.

"Do it," Kali said with a low growl. He could already see the beast's reluctance to do so much work. Kali wasn't having any of it. This was their home.

"Yes, Lord Kali." The gibbon bounded off on all-fours.

Filled with the knowledge he was going to have to oversee everything, Kali tried to rise once more, but the pain was so great that his vision filled with stars and he passed out.

***

Kali jolted awake when he sensed a nearby presence. He let out a warning growl as he lifted his head, which caused more pain to lance down his neck. The sun was up in full, rapidly warming the air. His leopards backed away, revealing Kali's brother Ashoka, covered in mud, accompanied by four, equally muddy otters who stood a respectful distance behind his tail.

"Ashoka," Kali said unhappily. "What are you doing here? How did you cross the river?"

"It's good to see you, too, brother," Ashoka said patiently. "I'm relieved to see you and your tribe alive. That storm has forever changed the landscape and the future of our tribes. And, to answer your question, I had help." He glanced at the otters.

"What do you want?" Kali said flatly. He had no time for this. He had to get up and dig out his village. He suspected that nothing had been done while he'd been unwillingly resting.

"I noticed your tribe is trying to dig out the village. The mud is deep and they are not getting far." Ashoka noted.

"That's because I haven't been able to get over there to tell them how to properly dig it out."

"With all due respect, brother, our homes are lost."

"That's what you think. Our homes are right here. We *will* get them back."

Ashoka slowly shook his head. "If a mudslide has struck here once, then it will strike again. Think of you and your tribe's safety. It's time for us to find a new place to call home."

"And where do you plan on taking your tribe?" Kali said smugly.

Ashoka turned and looked downriver to the ravine that lined both their villages. "We will find a way across that ravine. There is a nice-looking bit of jungle on the other side. It is more than good enough for all of us to call home." He turned back to his brother. "I suggest you do the same, but that's your choice."

"You're right. It is my choice, and we will stay."

Ashoka inclined his head deferentially and padded off in

the direction of Kali's tribe.

Kali cautiously tried to rise, but even the smallest amount of weight on his back paws caused awful pain. He let his belly sink on the grass. His legs were just as muddy as his brother's and they could both almost pass for brown panthers with a hint of stripes under the muck. "Where do you think you're going? You're going the wrong way," he called after his brother.

"That's what you think," Ashoka said in his calm voice that only further infuriated Kali.

The tiger lord watched helplessly as Ashoka trotted up to where the grassy hill ended and the thick mud began with his otters following close behind. All animals, big and small, were hopelessly trying to remove mud from the village. They had created mounds in places and even dumped mud off in the grass. Despite all that had been done, not one thatched roof had revealed itself. They all paused and looked up as Ashoka approached.

Ashoka stood proudly and raised his head. "Your efforts to reclaim your home are noble, but your efforts would be better spent finding a new place to call home." His strong voice effortlessly filled the air and reached every ear. "If you wish to move on, then I invite you to come with me. You will be welcomed into my tribe with open arms, minds, and hearts. Together we can build a new home in a safer place. The choice is yours."

Ashoka studied Kali's tribe a moment before padding off. His otters faithfully followed behind him. They veered towards the ravine and turned to a patch of mud where branches and leaves had been arranged around a piece of tree to form a path. With the help of a vine, the otters guided their lord across the river and continued on to join their tribe. All the animals could now cross the log without fear of being washed away.

Kali's tribe watched Ashoka's departure with indecisive longing, and then a few animals got up and followed. Other tribe members watched their comrades leave. Many exchanged looks amongst each other, and then followed as well.

The sight angered Kali, but when he saw the rhinoceros family and their calf take off after Ashoka, the tiger lord grew furious. The pain almost kept him from rising, but his rage helped him lurch onto unsteady paws. He wobbled. The pain was so bad that he felt sick to his stomach, but he swallowed and let out a roar. "Where do you all think you're going?"

A few looked at him but they all continued onward without faltering.

"We're leaving," an elephant said in a tone of finality. His trunk was covered in mud, as were his thick legs.

"No, you're not. Get back here. I did not give any of you permission to leave."

"We're not your tribe anymore. We don't need your permission for anything."

If they had already made up their minds that they were no longer his tribe, then there was nothing Kali could say or do to prevent them from leaving. But the rhino family...his anger rekindled. "I saved your calf! How dare you leave after what I did for you?"

The mother rhino stopped and swung her head to face him. Her ears pricked forward as she cooly stated, "It was because of you and your decisions that our calf was put in a position to need saving. Good day."

Kali wanted to point out that, if they'd moved faster, then they would have been out of harm's way, but a seed of doubt planted in his mind. If they had fled the village as soon as the water started rising, they would have been on the hillside long before the first rumblings began.

Despite recognizing the truth in her words, Kali's pride was still hurt. "You'll find that his tribe is nowhere near as good as mine. You'll see that this is a mistake."

"It was a mistake to stay here so long," the father rhino

said. "Ashoka is a good lord who loves and trusts his tribe. We haven't been happy for a long time. We are not loved or trusted by you. We are not leaving because of the mudslide. We are leaving because of you."

All the rage left Kali. He was defeated. He sat on his back legs as the rhino's words sank in. They were leaving because of him? How could this be? "You're lying," he said weakly.

"He's not," a mother civet said, her mate and family following beside her. "We are all leaving for the same reason." More animals chimed in, voicing their agreement.

Nearly half of Kali's tribe abandoned the fruitless attempt to unearth their village and instead traversed across the log and churning river that was now beginning to recede. The tiger lord watched helplessly as they left. Many glanced at him as they passed, but no one said anything. The anger and hurt on their faces were plain enough. If it had been there this whole time and he'd just never seen it? Maybe he'd been too busy being angry instead. He thought they were all just lazy and uncaring, yet they'd tried to dig out the village while he was unconscious.

Still, as many animals left, a few headed toward Kali. At first, he thought his tribe was coming to their senses and returning, but he quickly realized that he didn't recognize any of the sloth bears, panthers, or bengal monitor lizards plodding through the mud. A few of Kali's now former tribe members warned the newcomers to turn around, but the creatures ignored their words.

The sloth bears made it up the hill and bowed their heads, but the two leopards guarding Kali stepped between them. "Lord Kali," one sloth bear said. "Word has it you wish to remain here and rebuild your village."

"We are," Kali said with a nod.

The sloth bears looked up, their eyes widening with joy. "Then may we join your tribe? Lord Ashoka intends to cross the ravine and build a new village on the other side. However, we do not want to leave. Can we join you?"

"Of course. Welcome to my tribe." He looked out over the mud and grass, both of which were beginning to dry up as the sun climbed higher in the sky. What was left of his tribe worked on digging out a hut in the mud. They had made some progress, but their work had only just begun. He turned back to his new tribe members. "There is much work to be done to reclaim our home. Go join the others."

***

Eventually, Kali found the strength to move closer to the worksite. He collapsed at the edge as the pain dragged him to the ground, but he was still able to keep his head up and yell orders and directions. However, despite his tribe's best efforts, the worksite grew more chaotic and confused as time passed. If only he could move properly, Kali thought to himself, this would all be going so much better.

His tribe worked together in an attempt to remove a fallen tree but the mud held it firmly in place. A dozen larger animals tugged to pull it free, but only a portion of trunk snapped off as a result of their efforts. Kali snarled at them to pull it a different way. An elephant lost her footing and fell, knocking over a water buffalo and scattering the smaller animals in the process.

Kali yelled at the useless lot of them, scolding them for not being able to follow directions or get anything done. As soon as he stopped to catch his breath, every last animal that had once belonged to Ashoka's tribe, got up and climbed out of the mud.

"You are as awful as they said you were," one sloth bear said. "We're leaving. Staying here is not worth the tyranny."

Let them think what they want, Kali thought. They were just as bad as his own tribe. How did Ashoka get anything done with them? "You think you will be welcomed back so easily!?"

"Yes," a panther said firmly. "Lord Ashoka discussed the decision with us. He warned us that we may not like what we find over here, but he didn't explain what he meant. He also said this was a lesson we were going to have to learn on our own, but, once we learned it, he would gladly welcome us back. He values what we add to his tribe."

"What kind of leader lets his tribe make such choices?"

"One that values us and understands that we all must learn things. Sometimes, there are many ways to learn a lesson. We consider our lesson learned. Goodbye and good luck."

"Good riddance," Kali said bitterly.

And now his tribe was even smaller than before. Between needing to hunt, gather, and dig out the village, Kali realized there weren't enough animals to do all the work. This was going to take far too long. He looked up the mountainside. And if a mudslide happened again, their efforts would be for nothing.

Ashoka's tribe was clustered at the edge of the ravine, all of them gathered like they were discussing something as a group. Not one of them had spent a scrap of energy trying to dig out their own village. They really were going to leave it.

Kali painfully sat up. The mud was thick and the river, while still receding, had no clear bank to mark where the edge of the village should be. Based on the wide range of the mudslide, there was no telling what new path the river would make once it returned in full. The landscape had been forever changed in just one night.

The jungle on the other side of the ravine was lush, green, speckled with vibrant colors, and full of life. There was even an open space to build a new village and no mountainside for a mudslide to spill down. It was a very nice-looking jungle, to be honest.

Kali turned back to what remained of his tribe. A few still dug in the mud, but the rest watched him with muddy faces, waiting curiously. "Stop digging," he said in a resigned voice. The last few macaques paused in their efforts and then faced him when they sensed his resignation. "This place is no longer fit to be our home. My injuries have forced me to watch, but they also have allowed me to see that this place is no longer safe to build a village. A better, safer place awaits us on the other side of the ravine." He held his head as high as the pain would allow, wincing on the inside as the next words left his lips. "It's time to build a bridge."

CHAPTER 4
Building Bridges

It took a lot for Kali to swallow his pride and accept the fact that it was in their best interest to abandon their home for a new one, but he noticed his announcement sent a ripple of relief through his tribe. He ordered a pair of eagles to fly over to Ashoka and not only inform him of his decision to help build a bridge, but also demand the tiger lord order Kali's former tribe members to return to their former lord. Kali and the remainder of his tribe rested while anticipating the return of the other tribe members. All of them were tired from the hours of fruitless digging.

None of them returned, though. Instead, Lord Ashoka traversed the drying mud and scattered river in order to speak with Lord Kali. His fur was still caked in mud, but he looked overjoyed. Kali stood at his brother's arrival. He could move a little quicker, but even the slightest twitch still hurt and his legs trembled.

Ashoka said, "Your eagles brought me wonderful news, yet

I still see no bridge is being built."

"Return my tribe members to me. We need them. There are too few of us."

The joy left Ashoka's face. "They don't want to return."

Kali flattened his ears. "They won't or they can't?"

"Won't. I gave them permission to leave, but every last one refused. Brother, I suggest we speak in private. I think there are things you should know."

Kali looked at his tribe and then nodded to his brother. He tried to walk, but the pain in his legs caused him to stumble. After attempting to regain his balance, Kali dropped back onto the grass.

"Leave us," Ashoka ordered firmly, yet without any harshness in his voice. Without a word, the animals headed farther uphill, leaving the two tiger lords alone. Ashoka settled down on the grass so they lay eye-to-eye. He let out a slow sigh through his nose and gave his brother a measured gaze. "What happened to you?" he said, voice full of concern.

Kali looked away. "I saved a rhino calf that is now a part of your tribe. The river swept me under and debris battered me as I kept its head above water. I don't know what happened but I woke to a few tribe members watching over me. I can barely move."

"At least you are alive, and for that I'm grateful. I can have some birds bring you herbs for the pain, if you'd like. We have learned there are plants in the jungle that do more than look beautiful or offer sustenance."

Kali dug his claws in the dirt and grass. "I will not be seen taking aid from another tribe... not even yours."

"As you wish, Lord Kali," Ashoka said, voice full of disappointment. "My heart breaks with what I must reveal to you, but they must be revealed or I fear you will become tribelesse."

Kali narrowed his eyes. "Is that a threat?"

"No. It is a warning. I wish to help you. Your former tribe

members painted a terrible picture of what it was like to live under your rule. Will you listen to what I have to say?"

"And why do you care to help me? Aren't you happier to have so many tribe members under your rule?"

"You are my brother, not my enemy. Your tribe needs you to be a great lord. Again, will you listen to what I have to say?" When Kali remained quiet, Ashoka said, "Do you trust me to help you?"

"No. You are here for your own personal gain. You—"

"So then you truly trust no one but yourself." Ashoka frowned. "I'd hoped it was a falsehood. What happened? You are not the same brother I grew up with."

Kali frowned. "No one seems capable of earning my trust. Everyone disappoints me one way or another, even you."

"And you disappoint me, Kali," Ashoka said.

Kali opened his mouth to retort, but paused. "How?"

"Let me ask you a few questions, and then I'll explain how."

"Fine." He scarcely stopped himself from baring his fangs. His brother was being as annoying as when they were cubs.

"Who are the leaders among your tribe?"

"I am the sole leader. Why?"

"How does your tribe achieve goals?"

"I tell them what to do. That should be obvious."

"So then how does your tribe achieve success?"

"They do what I tell them to."

"Lastly, who has a say in how the tribe is run?"

"Me and only me. They are not qualified to offer input."

"I see," Ashoka said with a grave nod.

"Where are we going with this?" Kali said impatiently. "As far as I can see you're just wasting my time."

"We are exploring the truth. And the truth is you are destroying your own tribe."

"They destroyed our tribe by leaving."

"They left because of you. Animals don't leave tribes

because of the tribe. They leave because of the tribe leader."

Kali snarled at the memory of what the rhino family had said to him. The words still stung. "Leave. Go back to your own tribe. Now." When his brother didn't move, Kali flattened his ears and bared his fangs. "Leave!" He roared.

"No," Ashoka said calmly.

Kali bellowed a roar that filled the air and sent birds flying out of the jungle. His tribe turned as one and froze in place, watching the tigers.

Ashoka only glanced at them as the last echoes of the roar died away. "Judging by your reaction, you know, in your heart, that I speak the truth."

Kali knew his brother was right, but he couldn't bring himself to admit the truth. Instead, he dropped his head on his paws and stared at the grass. "Leave me," he said in a subdued voice as the memory of half his tribe leaving played out in his mind.

"Not like this, dear brother. Not like this. You are a lord and a tiger. I want your own tribe to love and respect you as much as my own tribe loves and respects me. Can I trust you to listen?"

Kali let out a sigh. "What's left to lose, besides the rest of my tribe?"

"Think of what you have to gain, instead." When his brother made no resistance to listen, Ashoka sat up. "When it comes to tribe leadership and management, there are six principles that separate a thriving tribe from one that flounders. These principles can help a tribe become stronger even during the worst times. However, if ignored, even a large tribe will fail when times get hard."

"How do you know this is true?"

"Before I began my tribe, I met with other tribe leaders, learned to do as they do, and made a note of what worked and what didn't. Over a few years, I found six universal principles that create a strong, collaborative tribe."

"So that's what you were doing after we went our separate ways?"

Ashoka nodded. "Since I have much to tell you about these universal principles and you have a bridge to build, I will break this into six pieces, six trials, that empower you and bring out your best. My first trial for you is trust."

"Trust?" Kali sat up and winced in pain.

"Yes, trust. Your tribe members give you their trust the moment they join. They trust you to provide them with safety and security, a place to belong and contribute to the overall wellbeing of the tribe, and to grow themselves and help the tribe grow.

"You say no one has been able to earn your trust. Yes, trust is earned, but it is also given. You have given your tribe no chance to build and earn your trust. This is why you struggle to thrive. I challenge you to learn to trust your tribe, starting with getting your bridge built. As their lord, you're going to have to take the first step. They have learned not to trust you. They need your trust as much as you need theirs."

"And what will trust get me?"

Ashoka smiled. "Try it and you will see. Send a bird my way when you have learned. In the meantime, my tribe has its own bridge to build. I am trusting you to take this lesson to heart. Now, it's up to you to validate my trust." He rose, the smell of crushed grass rising with him. "I look forward to seeing what happens. And I will give you one hint: if you look closely, you'll see that each of them is a tiger in their own right, too." He began heading back to his own tribe.

Kali sat a long while, absorbing all that had been said and reflecting on all that had happened. For a while he despaired, unable to see how he could possibly trust anyone without them earning it first, but his own brother had placed trust in him to achieve an impossible task.

Well, laying there and despairing wasn't going to get the

bridge built and his tribe to a safer place. He stood and called his tribe over. They were most certainly not all tigers but Kali set aside the thought. He had this trust thing to figure out and a bridge to build.

What remained of his tribe gathered in a semicircle around him, their faces full of wariness. Witnessing two tigers, two lords, have a mild argument was probably terrifying to them. A full-fledged argument would have involved teeth and claws, but what did they know about being tigers?

If you look closely, you'll see that each of them is a tiger in their own right, too.

Kali pushed the thought aside a second time. Why it kept coming back with persistence, he didn't know or care. He took in his mud-covered tribe and for once felt grateful they were still there. He couldn't be a lord without a tribe. Now, how was he supposed to trust them? He rose onto unsteady paws. "A few things have come to my attention these last few hours. First, as much as I'd like to stay here, we can no longer call this place home. It's dangerous. It's not worth the effort to dig out. Second, there is a very nice piece of jungle on the other side of the ravine. It lacks a mountain, and, therefore, also lacks the risk of being hit by a mudslide. Yes, it will still pose the usual dangers, but we already know how to manage those."

A king cobra slithered forward and bobbed its head.

Normally, Kali would be annoyed by a tribe member wishing to speak while he was talking, but he bit back his annoyance. "Yes, Kravel?"

"Lord Kali, I agree we need to move on, but a ravine lies between us and the new jungle."

"We are going to build a bridge," the tiger lord said calmly. "Lord Ashoka is doing the same. It will be beneficial in the long run to have a friendly neighboring tribe like we've had all these years." Many heads bobbed agreement. Kali clenched his jaw at the thought of what he was going to say next. He wouldn't have bothered saying anything if he hadn't seen the truth in his brother's words. His brother's tribe flourished while Kali's struggled to make ends meet daily. He wasn't happy, and clearly his tribe felt the same.

He took a deep breath. "It has also come to my attention that this tribe might be lacking trust. Is it true that not one of you trusts me as your lord and leader?"

The animals looked between each other, eyes wide, but they exchanged nods, building courage as a group. they voiced the answer Kali had hoped wasn't true.

The truth stung, but his mother had not raised her cubs to be cowards. If this was the truth, then he would face it head-on. He wanted to keep believing that it was all his tribe's fault for there being no trust, but trust flowed both ways. They had to earn it and so did Kali. Since they did not trust him, he clearly had done something to help create this situation. "As your lord, I will take the first step in fixing this." He took a deep breath, batting away the mounting panic in his chest. This was completely the opposite of what he was used to, but what he was used to wasn't working. "There needs to be trust if we are to be a happy, strong tribe, and if we're going to safely cross the ravine. I place my trust in every last one of you to build a bridge that will get us all safely across. Do you accept?"

His tribe gave him wide-eyes stares once again, but the energy they gave off was pure shock. There was no fear; just shock and a twinge of distrust. An elephant raised a large foot, indicating she wished to speak. "Lord Kali, let us gather the best trees to build this bridge. Give us this chance and we will not disappoint you."

Considering that he was too injured to oversee every last tree they chose, he was going to have to trust them. Kali hated this, but he had no choice. His throat tightened. "Do it," he said with a nod.

The elephants turned to head off, but an eagle named

Thenca said, "Wait! How do you know which will be the best trees if you don't know how long they need to be?"

An elephant with a broken tusk named Roose stopped. He said, "What does it matter so long as we have enough trees?" The elephants started heading off again.

"Thenca is right," Kali called after them. "You will only make more work for yourself. Let's think this through." He had to admit he hadn't thought of what Thenca said, but there was merit in it. The mudslide would make food hard to come by, especially kills for the carnivores. The less energy they expended to get this bridge built, the better.

Thenca flapped her wings and perched atop a water buffalo's horn. "We can carry vines across the ravine to measure the gap. Then we will know how long the bridge needs to be."

Animals voiced their approval.

A crested hawk-eagle hopped onto the water buffalo's other horn. "That is a good idea but the ravine's width varies from place to place, and who knows what the storm did to the integrity of edges?"

The building excitement died. An otter said, "So then do we abandon the bridge idea?"

Kali glanced at the ravine and caught a glimpse of Ashoka's tribe busying themselves with trees and bridge making. "No. We build a bridge in the safest place. This ravine has been here far longer than this tribe and has weathered many storms. It is strong."

Water buffalo and more elephants offered to test the edge of the ravine for stability, and Kali immediately set them to task. As much as he wanted to oversee their efforts, his inability to do much beyond standing would only put him at risk and make him a burden.

More and more ideas popped up as the plan to build a bridge developed. At first, Kali forced himself to listen to everyone's ideas and concerns, but the more things other animals thought of things that he didn't, the more eagerly he listened to their input. By the time the elephants and water buffalo had found and marked the safest part of the ravine, the bridge plan had been fully thought out and ready to put into action. Every animal had a job to do and everyone set off in several directions to either collect supplies or gather food and drinkable water.

Unable to contribute, Kali plopped back on the grass and watched everything from a distance. His trust was still shaky, but so was theirs. Still, they moved with an energy and enthusiasm he had not seen in years. Was this the result of trust? He hoped so.

CHAPTER 5
Trust Is Like an Oil

D erek stuck a bookmark complete with a pink tassel at the end of the chapter and closed the book. That's where the teacher said in the directions to stop, and now they had a worksheet to fill out, complete with line drawings of the animals from the book. His heart pounded as if it was trying to escape from his chest. The book seemed to be a metaphorical mirror to his office life. Was he really the same as this Kali character? A sinking feeling in his gut confirmed his suspicions.

Raven's eyelids were heavy with sleep, but she wore a faint smile. Martha said, "So what do you think of the story so far?"

Raven sat up between them. "I'm sad all the animals lost their homes and they can't get them back."

"Me, too," said Martha.

Derek scanned the worksheet, and then read the directions. It instructed parents to go over the questions one-by-one with their child and record their thoughts.. There were several questions including ones specifically for the parents. "The first question asks, 'Should Kali's tribe have escaped to safety as soon as Ashoka's tribe did? Why or why not?'"

Before he could voice his response, Raven said, "Yes, because it was dangerous."

"Dangerous?"

"Yeah, dangerous to stay."

"What made it dangerous?" Derek asked, the second question on the sheet.

She thought a moment. "The mudslide. It almost got Lord Kali, because he had to help the baby rhino."

Derek nodded and moved on to the third question. "Why did the animals leave Lord Kali?"

"He was being mean and making them dig out the village."

Suddenly, Derek saw himself at the office, yelling at his staff to move faster, to do a better job, the wide-eyed stares, and the gazes glued to the carpet floor. He'd been trying to make everyone meet deadlines, but, no matter what he told them to do, they acted as though they were stuck in the mud. All the work they did was going nowhere. Lord Kali clearly should have made some different decisions. Was Derek this tyrannical and forceful? Was he leading them nowhere? In the wrong direction?

A hand touched his shoulder. Martha gave him a meaningful look, and then nodded toward the worksheet. She must have seen the thoughts on his face.

Taking a deep breath, Derek zeroed in on the final question meant for the students. "Was it right for Lord Kali to yell at the animals who left his tribe? Why or why not?"

"No," Raven said. "It was mean. Lord Ashoka is nice. That's why they went to him instead."

John said in his exit interview that he left because of you.

Derek had been trying to get people to stop whining and just do their job. He had his own work to do and all the interruptions he suffered through on a daily basis weren't helping anyone, much less him. Maybe, like the civet family that had warned Kali it was time to seek higher ground, his employees were trying to tell Derek something, too. He'd just been too engrossed in his own work and deadlines to hear the truth of the situation. "What was the first trial about?" Derek said, reading from the worksheet.

"Trust," said Raven. "Lord Kali has to learn to trust his tribe if he is going to be a good tiger lord."

"Correct. And how did Lord Kali's tribe members feel when Lord Kali said he was going to start trusting them?" Derek had zero trust at the office—at least he had a strong hunch that his employees felt that way.

"They were unsure, but then they got so happy," Raven said with a smile. "They couldn't wait to start stuff they needed to build a bridge."

That was true, Derek thought. At first they were wary. They didn't know if they should believe Kali or not, but they responded quickly to their lord's honesty. The meeting exposed different perspectives and strategies that Kali didn't think of himself. Was this the value of teamwork and team perspective, along with critical thinking?

All of Derek's new employees started with gusto, but, within three months, every last one of them lost their drive. He thought they had merely become stressed about the job. It had never crossed his mind that he was the cause of their unhappiness.

Raven settled down and both parents took turns kissing her goodnight before retiring to the living room. Derek put a baseball game on for some background noise and took one look at his cell phone before setting it face down on the coffee table. He had eerily few emails awaiting his attention. Martha settled down on the couch beside him. They both sank a little lower as Derek centered the worksheet on one of Raven's hardcover books.

Martha said, "What do you think of the book so far?"

Removing the cap on his Sharpie pen, Derek stared unfocused at the worksheet. "I'm like Lord Kali, aren't I?"

"What leads you to believe that?" she said patiently.

Derek went on to describe his habit of not really listening to anyone and constantly sending people away with a few stern words when they needed help. Derek wanted everything done his way. His employees tried to deliver, but he'd interpreted their confusion as incompetence; not a request for help. "I don't need clones. I need a team. And, to build a team, I need to be a better boss and project manager."

Martha gave him a kiss on the cheek. "I know you can do it."

"This is humiliating," Derek blurted. "Did you think I was like Kali this whole time?"

"Definitely not to his degree," she said, resting her head on his shoulder. The subtle hint of roses filled Derek's nose. An ease only his wife could instill in him relaxed some of the tension in his aching back. Martha said, "But I suspected you weren't innocent in the overall dynamic. It's not easy being a good boss and it's not like everyone automatically knows how to be a good boss just because they get the position. It takes time to learn who you are as a boss, who your employees are as a team, and how to unify all that under your leadership. Don't be too hard on yourself. It's not like you wanted to be anything less than a good boss."

Heaving a sigh, Derek nodded. He filled out his and Martha's names on the worksheet and read the directions:

Dear parents,

Thank you for working with your student on this book. I am a firm believer that this book is a great learning tool for both adults and children. I've taught with it for over two years now and the overwhelmingly positive results always inspire me, filling my heart with joy. I hope you get as much out of it as previous families have.

The goal of this lengthy assignment is teaching children the core principles of teamwork and great leadership. It will help them lead and complete group projects. The sooner people learn them, the sooner these traits become a way of life. Through this third grade class, these principles manifest as stronger teamwork and a class of children eager to help each other. They lift each other up, instead of encouraging cutthroat competition for the top spot. I have even seen families become closer, which is an outcome I had not originally anticipated.

When completing this assignment, all I ask is that you not look at *The Tiger Lord's Trials* as just a children's book, but as a learning tool. I look forward to hearing how all of you become TIGERS. The following is a list of questions to stimulate thoughts and ideas.

Sincerely,
Mrs. Walters

Derek let out a thoughtful grunt. "Interesting."

"I know, right?"

The worksheet listed eight questions, each of them with space to record an answer. Derek set Sharpie pen to page and began filling it out.

1. Was it the storm's fault or Lord Kali's fault that the tribe was in so much danger?

Lord Kali's. He should have led them to safety once the water started rising.

2. What could have Lord Kali done differently to make his tribe safer?

Not only listen to his tribe members when they voiced concern, but also swallow his pride when he realized the rising water was a real problem.

3. Why was progress with digging out the village so terrible?

There was a ton of mud and no one had any real direction on where to dig, much less a goal location to start.

4. What was the cause of Lord Kali's tribe struggling to provide food and water?

He was the problem. Everyone was afraid of him and appeared to essentially feel like a slave under his tyranny. They had become dependent and didn't do anything he had not sanctioned, not even the repair of their roofs.

5. Does Lord Ashoka give his tribe members too much freedom? Why or why not?

At this point, it's hard to say. We haven't heard anything bad about the tribe. My knee-jerk reaction is that's way too much freedom, but then I don't trust people like he does. Maybe more trust like that is better. I just don't know

yet. Kali definitely doesn't give enough freedom.
No one believes in themselves to do a good job. No
one knows how to do their job well. No one knows
how to make decisions for themselves. Kali has
to do everything and it drags everyone down.

6. **What are your thoughts on trust being a core principle when it comes to leadership and teamwork?**

It sounds like trust has to be there to make things
work. Without it, no one knows what to do or if
they should do certain things. It seems to destroy
motivation when trust is absent. Perhaps trust is
like a very fine oil that keeps an engine running
smoothly when teams encounter anger and
disappointment.

7. **Where in your life do you think trust might be lacking?**

Derek let out a pitying laugh after reading the seventh and final question. Part of him wanted to leave it blank, to avoid facing the truth, but he had to take care of his family and salvage his job. When he'd first started years ago, he'd had the same fire as his new hires. It had been a dream job. Now, it was a nightmare of his own making.

Martha glanced at the worksheet and gave his arm a reassuring squeeze before turning her attention back to the baseball game.

Taking a deep breath to steel himself, Derek answered the final question.

As the boss of a team of employees, I've noticed there isn't a drop of trust left at the office. There are probably other areas of my life that need more trust, but work is at the forefront of my thoughts right now. My wife had a feeling that I wasn't doing something right at the office, but, either out of fear of upsetting me or feeling it was disrespectful, she said nothing, I just learned of it tonight.

Derek wanted to write more, but he ran out of room. He capped his pen. "I really have no trust at the office," he said softly.

"So, what do you want to do about it? Do you think you can salvage the situation or do you think you should move on? Do you even want to salvage it?"

Honestly, it was very tempting to just up and walk away from it all. Let the project be someone else's problem. However, whether it was his pride or determination, he couldn't bring himself to quit. It felt like giving up. Derek didn't want to take anything away from Martha's business or put them in a tough financial situation. "I have to fix it."

"I'm glad to hear that. I'm proud of you. I'll help you in any way I can." Placing a hand on his chest, she snuggled deeper against his side.

Derek placed a hand over hers and sat up straighter. "Yes, I'm going to need all the help I can get." He moved on to the final question.

8. What makes trust fail and what makes it work?

Mrs. Walters included a T-chart of responses.

WHAT MAKES IT FAIL	WHAT MAKES IT WORK
• Saying one thing and doing another	• Modeling the behavior you want to see in others
• Expecting behaviors you don't reciprocate	• Trying to do the right thing
• Abusing or neglecting resources of others	• Being open and transparent
• Being unpredictable	• Becoming better at what you do
• Striving for personal benefit at the expense of others	

Derek was most certainly guilty of all the above in the left column. At least he was aware of it, now. He flipped over the page and created his own T-chart.

Reasons why employees don't trust me	How to do things differently to fix that
• Yell	• Talk to them; not at them
• Get angry	
• Don't listen	• Stay calm
• I don't help them	• Actually listen
• They don't know how I'm going to act	• Help them if they get stuck
• I don't trust them	• Make behaviors/ actions predictable
• I don't know them personally	• Give them a chance to validate my trust
	• Begin talking with my employees to get to know them and what motivates them

Yes, changes like this would help build trust if it wasn't too late. "I think this is everything I'm doing to make everyone distrust me. I'll have to talk to them individually to make sure." Hopefully, they'd be honest after all they'd been through.

Well, there was the first step of his action plan to turn things around. Derek tossed and turned all night, unable to shut off his brain and stop thinking about the book. He fell asleep sometime after 3 am, but dutifully rose at 8 am to tackle a day of chores and helping with Raven. He remained pensive and quiet most of the day. And his wife left him in peace, until night two of book reading began.

CHAPTER 6
When Two Heads are Better Than One

Kali must have dozed off at some point. When he opened his eyes again, a huge stack of muddy trees, several piles of vines, and fresh food lay before him. His tribe had collected bridge building supplies while he slept and now looked at him expectantly. Some grazed on nuts and berries, and a few birds circled overhead.

One of his leopards said, "The supplies await your inspection, as you requested."

His stomach growled at the sight of the food, but breakfast would have to wait. He slowly stood and discovered that he could finally move a little easier, but the pain was still constant. He gingerly made his way to the fallen trees and gave them a sniff. He swatted at one and it held. He swiped harder, causing pain to lance from paw to shoulder, but the tree remained in one piece. It bore three lines from his claws and nothing more. He tested a few more trees despite the pain. He couldn't afford to show weakness, not when he was trying something new as a lord. To his relief, every last tree passed his strength test. He even had an elephant squeeze one with its trunk and step on it. The tree held under the pressure.

Kali nodded in grudging approval. "You did well," he said in a low, unhappy voice. His tribe had managed to do something right without him overseeing the whole process. Was it truly his fault—and not theirs—that the tribe had struggled to adequately feed and water themselves all this time because of his leadership? "These trees are strong. They will make a good bridge." He didn't want to believe it. With just half a tribe, everyone had accomplished their work so quickly and efficiently. Kali had left them alone to do their jobs, and they had done very well.

With all the materials gathered, it was time to build.

Birds and gibbons worked together to stretch out the vine that measured the width of the ravine and the elephants began laying out tree trunks alongside it. Civets, macaques, and other smaller creatures, capable of carrying vines in mouths or paws, constantly got underfoot and slowed the elephants' progress. One macaque even got its tail stepped on, halting everything until the ripple of panic settled down and the macaque was removed from vine duty.

Kali impatiently ordered his tribe around, trying to keep all the smaller animals out of harm's way and also direct the elephants to lay the trees where they needed to go. Progress slowed and grew more confused, and Kali grew more frustrated. The whole operation went from the entire tribe moving supplies around and putting things in place, to just a few animals working and only moving after Kali had told them what to do. By the time the sun started sinking in the west, they had some semblance of a bridge. However, one test step from Bhari the elephant and the whole thing fell apart. Vines snapped, trees rolled out of position and animals scattered to avoid getting crushed by both tree and elephant alike.

"Useless, all of you!" Kali growled, limping as he tried to

pace. There was nothing worse in the jungle than feeling restless yet unable to move. He could barely manage two steps in any direction before pain overwhelmed him. "I put my trust in all of you and you failed me." Heads sank and smaller animals disappeared into the grass or behind bigger animals. "My hopes rose when you gathered all the supplies we needed and even brought food back quickly, but you can't seem to follow my directions anymore. How am I supposed to trust you now?"

His tribe remained silent, which only further angered him.

A low, unidentified growl rippled through the air and the tribe froze. Kali looked in the direction the growl had come from and flattened his ears. Ashoka. "Now what do you want, brother?"

His brother looked at the unhappy tribe. "Go rest. You may return when we are done talking."

Kali would have charged his brother in that moment if he were capable. Instead, he could only fight Ashoka's disrespect with words. "They are not your tribe to order around."

Ashoka held his head proudly, tail tip casually flicking from side to side. "They probably will be if you do not get this bridge built. You started with trust, but it appears you forgot about it when it came time to build the bridge." He nodded to the animals and they departed, some more eagerly than others.

Kali watched in silence. The tribe's distrustful energy had returned. It had been going so well before it had reverted back to the unhappy, dysfunctional tribe he knew. Yet they'd had a moment of success. Why couldn't they get back to that?

As the last water buffalo walked out of hearing range, Ashoka said, "It appears you made some good progress. What happened with trust?"

Kali took in the mess that was supposed to be their bridge. "It worked and then it stopped. What good is trust if it's not consistent?"

"An excellent question, brother," Ashoka said as he stood

beside him and studied the mess. "What changed? Why did the flow of trust stop?"

"I don't know," Kali sighed. "They gathered adequate building material and that's the fastest they've ever gathered food. But, as soon they started building the bridge, everything became chaotic and one animal got stepped on! If they'd just follow my directions, we'd have a bridge by now."

"What are you telling them?" Ashoka asked quietly.

"Where to place trees, how to tie the vines, and so on. Everything." Kali shook his head.

"And who told them which trees to pick, which vines to gather, where to gather nuts and berries, and where to hunt for your food?" Ashoka nodded in the direction of what remained of the meal.

"They did all that themselves. I told them what needed to be done and they got it done while I rested." Kali's gaze snapped in his brother's direction and he narrowed his eyes. "Are you saying I'm the reason we don't have a bridge yet?"

Ashoka's lips curled in the smallest of smiles. "What drew you to that conclusion?"

Kali flexed his claws, digging into the ground. "Before all the bridge materials were gathered, we planned out what we needed as a tribe. Everyone was assigned a task, all of them related to getting the bridge built, and then they went off and did their jobs. I—" *reluctantly*, he thought but avoided saying it "—put my trust in them to get these tasks done and they validated my trust. We have all the materials we need, along with full bellies." He licked his chops, thinking of the meal he'd had not too long ago.

"So then what changed once you started building?" Ashoka inquired patiently.

"I started telling them how to get things done. I had to tell them to undo and keep redoing things over and over. We went from everyone working to just a few. And, well, you see how that ended up." He looked away, specifically at his tribe camped farther uphill. "What did I do wrong?" he said unhappily. This was humiliating. It was so much better when he believed he was right in blaming everyone else for the dysfunction.

" I know this isn't easy for you to willingly admit, brother, but I assure you these trials will bring as much success as the gathering of food and materials. You have validated my trust in you. Maybe you can become a great lord... even better than me." He looked at Kali. "You were catching up to our progress before your bridge fell apart."

Kali flinched. How could that happen? His tribe had such small numbers compared Ashoka's. How could Kali's tribe possibly build a bridge faster than his brother's?

"It's true. There is a great lord in you, waiting to be drawn out. And you have a tribe full of animals eager to bring out their inner tiger. You don't need a large tribe to accomplish great things; you just need a tribe where everyone is committed to the same goals."

"Our goal is to safely get across the ravine and build a new home."

"A good, clear goal," Ashoka said. "Your tribe members knew it, too, when they went off to hunt and gather supplies. Even gathering food and water supported the overarching goal to get a bridge built. When you left them alone to do their tasks, you gave them your trust and it resulted in food and supplies. When you started ordering animals around and micromanaging every last detail, you removed trust. Suddenly, no one could perform the smallest task without your input. Do you trust monkeys to be able to climb trees?"

Kali furrowed his brows, not understanding the purpose of the question. "Of course. That's what they're meant to be able to do."

Ashoka nodded. "So it would be silly for a tiger to tell a monkey where to place their paws as they climbed, wouldn't it?"

"Yes. Just let the monkey climb. He'll get up there." That would be beyond ridiculous to do, even if Kali was another monkey.

"Yes, let the monkey climb. Let your tribe members do the work they know how to do. You're trying to do everyone's job yourself when you step in like you did earlier. That's why progress nearly halted and the bridge fell apart. You stopped trusting your tribe members to do their individual jobs, and they stopped trusting you as a leader, once again."

"But how can I trust them if they don't know what to do... much less how to do it?"

"When you interfere and instruct them to do jobs they know how to do, no one starts working until you direct them. Now, since you know this and have had a taste of success with trust, I give you my next trial: interdependence. I'm sure you have already encountered that with the planning of the bridge."

"What is interdependence?" Not trusting resulted in work slowing down and that made sense.

"It is when you and your tribe work together to achieve goals with high levels of cooperation. It focuses on using each animal's unique strengths. You wouldn't have an eagle digging holes or expect a civet to fly. That would be silly. It's placing your tribe members in the right jobs so that they can successfully achieve a common goal. It is also about each tribe member trusting you enough to be honest about their strengths and weaknesses."

"Interdependence fosters the ability to work together and accomplish anything as a tribe. When everyone works to their strengths, appreciates everyone else's contributions to the goal, trusts each other, and works together, it enables every last tribe member to succeed. For example, your vines didn't hold. Who are the members of your tribe that know the most about vines? Certainly not you and me. When tribe members cooperate and do what they naturally know how to do, things get done faster. "

"More trust," Kali said unhappily.

"Just as everyone had a role earlier, you must give them a role again and allow them to fulfill it. Tribe members must trust each other to do their respective jobs. This trial isn't for you alone. It helps to ask them good questions that help them think, plan, and accomplish their plans. When they come up with their own solutions, under your guiding questions, you build cooperation and respect for individual strengths."

"Dependence is relying on others to give you directions. Independence is doing your job by yourself. Interdependence sounds like it takes more work, but things get done faster when you cooperate with others. This happens when you recognize each animal has strengths and you encourage them to work together from their strengths. You teach them interdependence. You lead by example and they follow. Do you understand?"

"Yes. I see the merit in your words." Kali studied the mess, picturing his tribe working together and constructing the bridge without anyone getting stepped on.

"Then why do you sound so disappointed?" Ashoka sounded more curious than upset.

"My way as lord hasn't been working," Kali admitted. "I have to change things. I have failed myself and my tribe."

"Every failure is a lesson. You are learning this now. We all make mistakes and have to learn from them. This is how everyone improves. These changes you're making will turn you and your tribe into a success with a clear goal and a ravine to cross."

"That it will," Kali said. The sun was sinking behind the jungle awaiting their arrival, casting long shadows that had yet to reach the ravine. He let out a resigned sigh, his pride leaving with it.

"You can do this, Kali. I believe you have just enough light to organize your tribe and reason through why your bridge broke before the sun sets. I will let you get to it. I will see you in the morning." Ashoka rubbed up against his brother, a gesture of affection and reassurance, and headed back to his tribe.

Kali took a moment to watch him depart before calling his tribe over with a gentle roar. As humiliated as he felt, he had to get his tribe across the ravine as soon as possible. He had to master this trust thing and see how interdependence would strengthen his tribe. Ashoka was right. Kali had to make sure everyone had an important role and allow them to fulfill their roles. It was a good lord's job to make sure everyone knew their role and how to best contribute to the goal.

The tribe approached him with hesitation. There was no fear in their movements, but the distrust was still there. They didn't know what to expect of Kali or what he wanted from them. No wonder they were so confused and wary. At least he was able to see it now and do something about it. Once the last frog settled down, Kali spoke.

"You all showed me that I could trust you by providing ample food and materials for a bridge. Now, I must extend that trust to building the bridge. In order to do that, every last one of you must have a clear role in this process. We have a plan for the bridge the gibbons drew for us. We know how long it needs to be, how strong our materials are, and where to place it once it's built. But first, we must decide roles in the building process."

"But Lord Kali," a macaque said, "we did build a bridge and it fell apart."

"I know the main reason why," Kali said patiently. "We will build it again and this time we will succeed." He sized up his tribe and began assigning roles to everyone. "I was the main reason why the bridge failed. All the other steps we should have taken before starting never took place." His animals looked at him blankly. "For example, the bridge collapsed when Bhari the elephant stepped on it. Why do you think that happened?"

His tribe stood there in silence, but the distant looks in their eyes assured Kali that they were sifting through their memories and thinking the moment over. A macaque tentatively raised a paw. "I think it broke because he was too heavy."

"Yes, but we're trying to build a bridge that can hold him and several elephants at once. Again, why did the bridge break?"

A second macaque stepped forward, wringing her little hands. "We didn't use enough vines and I don't think we did a good job of tying them well."

"And you would know since you spend much time among the vines and trees," Kali said.

"Yes, Lord Kali. We wanted to say something sooner, but you were too busy."

"Which is why we're going to plan this bridge out in full before we lay down another log. I need all of you to contribute your expertise on the materials we need to build the best, strongest bridge we can."

And contribute they did—so much so that it surprised Kali how knowledgeable they were on vines, trees, mud, sap and so on. He had no idea that so much knowledge was readily available to him. It took some time to put all the information together into one solid bridge plan, but it went faster than Kali anticipated.

The tribe decided that the elephants would place trees, buffaloes and bulls would move them around, gibbons and macaques would tie the trees together tightly, and the birds would monitor progress from above and call out adjustments as necessary. The smaller animals were tasked with gathering mud and sap to help strengthen the vines, and make sure everything stayed in place. Whomever Kali didn't give a direct bridge-building role was supposed to either hunt, gather more food, or patrol the territory for intruders. Just because the whole jungle had been hit by a storm, that wouldn't stop predators and opportunists from trying to make a meal out of any of them. On top of that, they would need the extra food to help keep them energized.

Enthusiasm returned. While trust was still uncertain, there was more hope. Now, they just had to act.

The tribe set to work. The food gathers bounded off into the jungle, and the guards found hidden places to keep an eye out. His animals tackled the bridge building with enthusiasm. What first looked like hasty chaos turned into an efficient system. The elephants and water buffalo moved around placing trunks under the helpful eyes of the eagles and hawks, while macaques, civets and other small creatures darted about with vines, mud and sap. A few times Kali opened his mouth to yell out a warning, but it was like his tribe instinctively knew where everyone was. They knew where to step without treading on tails or toes, or tripping up the larger animals. Trees were perfectly lined up, gibbons pulled vines tight with the help of elephants and water buffalo, and macaques and gibbons tied the vines into place. The bridge began to take shape as the sun set behind the distant jungle, casting them in twilight.

By the time it was too dark to work, the bridge was halfway done, and they had more food and water to fill their bellies. Kali ordered them all to rest for the night. He would have joined the leopards in patrolling the perimeter, but he still couldn't limp far. He curled up a slight distance from the rest of the tribe and shut his eyes.

CHAPTER 7
The Perks of Strong Leadership

Sunrise came way too early. Being a nocturnal creature, Kali usually let the sun rise and daily routines go on without him, until his need to oversee everything became too unbearable to ignore. However, this morning, he stirred with the first bird calls. The river was returning but, instead of one large line of water, it spread like a delta, flowing along its usual route and where both villages had been, wending around fallen trees and other debris. This location was undeniably lost to them.

The rest of the tribe woke as well, the smaller animals faster than the larger ones. The elephants, buffalo, macaques and gibbons in particular were quite sore, Kali learned from listening in on their morning chatter. He'd used his excellent hearing in the past to eavesdrop. This was still eavesdropping, but at least it was out of curiosity, instead of seeing if he needed to reprimand someone. The macaques' and gibbons' fingers were sore as well from all that vine tying. Still, they ate enough to get themselves going and returned to the bridge task.

Kali could move without limping, but his back and neck still hurt; his limbs had gone stiff overnight. He carefully arched his back and stretched his legs, but his strides remained short and tender. At least he could stand and move without fear of falling over. He padded over to the bridge-in-progress.

Animals stiffened as he approached. They tried to go about their work as if nothing was wrong, but Kali saw the stiff, jerky movements, and everyone's reluctance to make eye contact with him. Their movements grew hasty and sloppy. Kali snapped at them to slow down and pay attention to what they were doing. "Why are you all getting so nervous just because I'm here?"

Keshan, the gibbon clutched the vines he was supposed to be helping tie. "We're sorry, Lord Kali. We will do better."

Kali walked over and placed a paw on top of Keshan's vines. The gibbon looked up, eyes wide and full of terror, and his body froze. "That doesn't answer my question," he tried to say calmly, but an edge snuck into his voice. He removed his paw.

Keshan swallowed and his gaze dropped to his hands. Strong, stubby fingers wrung the vines. "I… we… Lord Kali, I don't want to be afraid, but I am. I mean no disrespect."

"You're afraid of me," he said with realization. "It's plain on your face and the energy you're giving off. Why are you afraid?" He understood his tribe's fear yesterday, after Kali had roared at his brother, but why now when they were making great progress?

Keshan looked at his fellow tribe members and lowered his gaze submissively. "You're always angry and critical. We don't know if we are doing it right, but we always hear when we do something wrong. It's hard to try." He said no more.

Kali stared in disbelief. He'd been angry lately due to having to deal with the storm, mudslide and injuries, along with a terrible first attempt at building a bridge. High stress and lots of physical pain would make anyone grumpy. His tribe had no reason to be afraid of him at the moment, yet they were.

"We're sorry, Lord Kali," Keshan said. He tried to go back to work but Kali put a paw on the vines again.

"Clearly I have taught you to be afraid." Fear and respect were two different things. His mother had taught both him and his brother that long ago. Kali hopped onto the completed half of the bridge, causing pain to shoot down his back, but he stood tall as he faced his tribe. "Stop what you're doing and listen to me a moment." The animals obeyed and a sea of faces looked up at him. The tiger lord took a deep breath. "When my brother and I were cubs, our mother taught us about respect. One thing that stuck out to me was that fear does not breed respect. It breeds resentment and distrust. I have been so focused on my anger and frustration that I didn't realize how much my fear of failing I'd instilled in you. This...this is not the tribe I want to create, or the tribe we are." Humiliation roiled through his chest. They were probably all about to get up and leave for Ashoka. Kali wouldn't blame them if they did. He realized it would be all his fault and not theirs. Now that Ashoka had made so much clear about why his tribe was the way it was, he could not deny this new revelation. "I did not realize how my actions and words have affected you all this time. I...I'm...sorry." And he meant it.

His tribe studied him in open wonder. Distrust kept them still.

Kali never spent time saying please or thank you, must less apologizing for anything. It was just order after order, telling everyone what to do, when to do it and how to get jobs done, and nothing had ever been good enough. He had been angry. A lot. And now Kali had a real glimpse of how his tribe saw him.

Keshan tentatively lumbered forward on all-fours. Head down, gaze lowered, he reached out and touched one of Kali's paws. "Thank you. Hearing that means a lot to me. Thank you. We will do better."

Kali looked at Keshan and suddenly his eyes stung. He blinked rapidly until his vision cleared. "You're welcome." More animals approached him and expressed their thanks one by one. The tiger lord became overwhelmed with their gratitude, but at the same time uplifted. He was genuinely sorry for making them so fearful, and they were genuinely grateful for his apology. The moment was like nothing he'd ever experienced as a lord, but it was good, despite the tightness in his throat and stinging in his eyes. There was a lightness filling his body, like he had just awoken from a good day's sleep. "Go ahead and continue with the bridge. I must go speak to my brother."

He slowly padded off across the river delta, leaving his tribe to do their work in peace. The mud had dried up everywhere, but near where water flowed. The trek was easy enough, the water rising no higher than his ankles, and no crocodiles or anacondas lay in wait to ambush a passerby. His body ached as he moved, but it wasn't anything he couldn't tolerate.

Kali glanced over his shoulder. Two elephants worked together to lay down the next tree as birds circled close overhead. His tribe fluidly worked together, their movements smooth and sure. Kali had created this picture just by making a few, simple changes.

Just the other day he was incapable of letting such a thing happen. He let out a small laugh, marveling at how many good things had stemmed from Ashoka's lessons. His tribe was happier, more efficient, and Kali—while still feeling humiliated if he thought about it too much—felt happier as well. This was turning out to be the tribe he always wanted, the tribe his animals wanted, too. He'd changed a little bit and his tribe had changed with him.

Eagles screeched alarm overhead as Kali approached Ashoka's tribe. Two leopards appeared out of the tall grass and flanked him, but said nothing as they led him deeper into their camp. One sniff and they knew who Kali was. His scent was almost identical to his brother's. Kali let himself be guided past the bridge-building commotion and straight to Ashoka.

The leopards scurried back to border patrol as soon as the two tigers were face-to-face, heading in the direction they'd come. The two tigers watched them a moment before facing each other.

Ashoka said, "Welcome, brother. This is a pleasant surprise. I'm glad to see you're moving better, too."

Kali nodded and plopped on the grass. He didn't care how submissive it made him look to his brother's tribe. The trek had been a couple of miles and now he ached all over. Ashoka's tribe gave him wary looks as they worked on a bridge that looked quite similar to his. It was close to done. "I have learned more things," Kali said.

"The interdependence went well?"

"Our bridge is halfway done. So, yes. But I come to you not about that, but about something else." He told him about the fears he'd instilled in his tribe members, the apology, and how his tribe reacted. Ashoka listened intently and nodded a few times.

"You truly have done well," Ashoka said. "I'm proud of you. My next trial for you was learning genuineness, but you are doing that already."

"Tell me more about it anyway. Why is it so important when it comes to being a good lord?" Yes, he'd seen some results of genuineness, but, if he were to remember to be genuine consistently, he needed to fully understand why.

Ashoka sat on his haunches and watched his tribe a moment. The animals moved just as fluidly as Kali's. Their bridge was nearing completion. Soon, all they would have to do was move it into place and cross it. "We creatures are good at sensing when someone is not being genuine. We smell it. But we are not always aware of it in ourselves. We get into the habit of responding to others with less than our truth, instead of being respectfully sincere, frank and forthright. Maybe some were taught as cubs not to trust the truth. Maybe fear and anger caused tribe members to do and say things to protect themselves that were less than truthful. They also need to relearn how to be respectfully sincere, frank and forthright without being afraid. We don't always consciously recognize it, but we sense it nonetheless and react to it. This impacts both trust and interdependence. Can you see that? Genuineness starts with a tribe's lord, and then it is up to the rest of the tribe to reciprocate genuineness. Not everyone knows how to commit to this and some will refuse because they have ulterior motives. Animals like these do not belong in the tribe."

"Have any of my former tribe members done this?" Kali said.

"Not yet at least," Ashoka said. "One or two may reveal a lack of genuineness over time, or none of them will. It is not always immediately apparent. Genuineness is telling the truth from your perspective, and giving and receiving clear feedback. It takes positive self esteem to be genuine. When your tribe members tell you what they think you want to hear, they are not being genuine. When our animals have to be different around us than with their families, they are not being genuine. I hope for and expect the best, but I am always prepared for the worst."

"How do you do that? How do you not live in fear that everyone is false and just here for their own personal gain?"

Ashoka nodded in understanding. "An easy trap for an inexperienced lord. Like I said, genuineness starts with you. From there, you will naturally attract like minds and get what you give. Genuineness has a habit of spreading. It fosters respect and commitment to you and the rest of the tribe. There will always be exceptions where some animals think they can take advantage of your genuineness, but they will weed themselves out. You will spot them and it becomes your responsibility to either help them find a tribe that better suits them, or just politely show them the way out. Don't let them stay. It tears apart an otherwise strong tribe, and your genuine members will come to resent you for not handling the situation. You will lose that genuineness. Protect those you value from those who don't value you and the rest of the tribe."

"I think I understand," Kali said. "I've never removed anyone from my tribe before. I think it was a matter of pride. If they joined, I wasn't letting them go. They were going to do what I told them to, and that was it. No one was allowed to leave." He watched the animals work on the bridge's construction, recognizing many of them as his former tribe members. "We see how well that worked out. Now my pride is even more injured."

"At least you have learned from it," Ashoka said encouragingly.

Kali gave a noncommittal shrug. He still had a lot to learn if something like this was not to happen again. A memory came to mind. "Once, we had a kingfisher in my tribe. His job was to hunt fish for us and guard the part of the river that ran along the village. He hunted mostly for himself and only produced fish when I got on his case. If I didn't berate and threaten him, he didn't produce fish. Other animals who fished as well complained to me about his laziness, but I always told them to worry about what they were doing. Their productivity went down and I got angry at all of them, including the kingfisher." Kali shook his head. "I see now that I should have removed the kingfisher from my tribe."

"He probably just wanted the perks of being in a tribe without giving anything back in return."

"Yes, unfortunately, but I was fixated on making him do what I wanted. The thought of removing him never crossed my mind." He let out a resigned sigh.

"At least now you know."

"At least now I know," Kali said softly. If only he could go back and fix it.

They chatted a bit more, changing the subject to Ashoka's bridge. His tribe had encountered problems of their own, despite trying to plan everything out and anticipate every possible challenge and danger. They'd restarted the bridge a few times as they found holes in their plans. Each time, they'd decided as a tribe to start over, but it had instilled confidence in themselves and their bridge.

Kali politely bid good day and wished Ashoka well on his bridge, and then pretended to be paying attention to what lay ahead of him while turning his head just enough to give his former tribe members a longing look. If only he'd done a few things differently, then they'd never have left. He was going to make sure this never happened again with the rest of his tribe.

He collected his thoughts as he made the two-mile trip back to his tribe. He couldn't show up feeling sorry for himself. He needed to be a lord and help get this bridge built in any way he could, even if it meant staying out of the way and letting them work in peace.

His tribe moved slower than yesterday. His paw-jerk reaction was to question the drop in productivity, but he stopped and observed first. His observations made him aware of the fang-flashing grimaces, tightness around eyes, and frequent licking of paws and fingers. His tribe was hurting, but not one of them complained. The nearest animals paused in their work only long enough to give him polite head bobs of welcome. He inclined his head in return as he quietly wandered among them, taking in their pain and progress, pausing now and then to ask questions and make suggestions instead of orders. He also praised his animals for doing something right and made it an example for others to follow. His animals listened and made the adjustments without any fear or resentment in their movements or energy.

The sun was brushing the awaiting jungle's canopy when the bridge was finally completed. The tribe gathered in a semicircle on one side to admire their handiwork.

Six overlapping tree trunks, three on each side and laying in a pattern like the side-to-side snake slither, ran the length of the vine that measured the ravine's gap. Atop those trunks lay a seemingly endless row of more trunks tightly lashed together. Two more trunks lined each side of the bridge to provide further stability and help keep animals a safer distance from the edge. Mud filled many gaps around the vines and between trunks, and sap made the vines shiny and strong.

Without saying a word, Kali approached the bridge and studied how the vines had been tied, tugging at a few with a flexed claw. They were tightly bound with no give. The trunks had been laid in a perfect, tidy row. The bridge height was as tall as Kali. Rearing up, he placed his paws on a trunk running the length of the bridge, feeling out how his back and legs would handle a small jump. His back was still stiff and sore, as were his legs, but he leapt anyway. His front legs cleared the tree with ease, but his back legs seized up and he hit the trunk with his back paws. A quick scramble got him up and over, but he left behind two sets of claw marks from catching himself. He glanced at his tribe. Their wide eyes calmed back to curious stares as Kali stood up straight despite the throbbing in his paws. He walked the length of the bridge. While he was fairly heavy, the bridge didn't creak in the least. It felt as solid and sure as stone.

"Habba," he called out and an elephant approached him. She had short tusks and big ears, and her trunk had been rubbed raw from all the labor. "Walk with me." He moved far enough down the bridge to allow her space to climb on.

Habba tested the ramp with a foot larger than Kali's head. The wood creaked, but held as she bore her weight down on it. Her massive frame rose higher and she stepped onto the bridge and stopped.

Kali could feel his tribe's worry from where he stood. Everyone held their breath, hoping the bridge was strong, but fearing it would suffer the same fate as their first one. They had worked so hard for so long, yet their efforts could be unraveled in an instant.

Habba took one step forward, and then another. The bridge groaned the slightest of creaks, but nothing shifted. Kali led her across and they both stepped off the other side without incident. Kali gave the bridge one last studious look and turned back to his tribe. "You all have done well—very well. The bridge is strong. This will work. I am genuinely pleased with all you have accomplished. Thank you."

Just like when he'd apologized, his tribe stared in open shock. And then, as his praise sunk in, a ripple of sound spread through the tribe. Macaques and gibbons hooted and cheered, elephants trumpeted, leopards roared, and water buffalo tilted their heads back and bleated. Eagles and hawks screeched overhead. The commotion grew louder as everyone fed off each other's energy. Every last sound was full of joy. A roar filled Kali's throat as their joy filled him. This was wonderful. This was perhaps the greatest success they'd had as a tribe. His animals were overjoyed and somehow that made him just as happy. He lifted his head and joined in their celebratory cries.

Kingfishers and hornbills flew off to spread the news of the complete bridge to those still patrolling and gathering food. "Lord Kali speaks praise," the birds cried. "The bridge is done and it is good. We have done well! Spread the word!" Their cries grew distant as they disappeared into the broken jungle.

Kali stood before his tribe. It took a long moment, but they calmed down enough to listen. They were wiggly and full of excitement, but they sensed his desire to speak and quieted their voices, nudging each other to quiet down. The tiger lord said, "Yes. Well done. I put my trust in all of you and you have shown me that you have been worthy of trust all this time. I thank you. You have also shown me that we can work together very well, and appreciate what each of us brings to the tribe. Everyone has their strengths and specialties, and now we have a strong, solid bridge because we combined all those strengths under a unified goal.

"Now, it is time for rest. You all bear the marks of hard labor. Rest up, eat well, and we will get the bridge in place tomorrow. You have earned this."

A bengal monitor lizard named Calum came forward, a forked tongue sticking out every few strides. He stopped before Kali and bobbed his long head. "Lord Kali, rain is coming. I can taste it in the air."

Kali sniffed the air and smelled no sign. He breathed deeper and could smell water, but he couldn't tell if it was just the river slowly returning or a foretelling of more rain, forcing him to trust that Calum spoke the truth.

"Would it be wiser to position the bridge now, instead of later?" Calum asked.

To be honest, it might. Who knew what toll more rains would take on their wounded land, but did his tribe have it in them at the moment to move something so heavy? Kali addressed the crowd, "Calum speaks of more rains coming. This leaves us with two choices: move the bridge now or rest up and move the bridge at first light. You are all tired and hurting and could use the rest, but at the same time we don't know what complications the rains will bring. Discuss as a tribe what you want to do. I will listen and give input, but since you are the ones who need to move the bridge, I am leaving this choice up to you. If there isn't a unanimous decision, we will go by majority choice."

His tribe closed into a circle with Kali in the middle and started discussing the pros and cons of each option. Kali slowly paced around the open space, listening, and then threw in the idea of recruiting former tribe members for help. They agreed they didn't have the numbers to take turns moving the bridge in groups. A crested hawk-eagle who flew to Ashoka and back delivered news that none of their former tribe members were interested in helping their former lord. Disappointment quieted them until Kali urged them to keep going. While he didn't outright apologize, he took full blame for their former tribe members' decisions.

They went back to deliberating their options.

Eventually, the general consensus was to wait until morning. They were all quite tired and in a fair bit of pain. It would be safer to move the bridge after some rest. Trying now would put them all at risk for injury and making mistakes. Then they'd have to try again either during or after the incoming rains. Several still wanted to start now, but they honored the majority decision and Kali saw to it that they all got some food and rest.

As much as they needed rest, he hoped it would be enough to overcome their next trials.

CHAPTER 8
Insights

D erek hastily but politely kissed Raven goodnight before hurrying off to the living room with the second worksheet and a notebook. So that's why the trust part had failed for a bit. Kali hadn't learned "interdependence". However, once he gave his animals a chance to flex their individual strengths, things started happening again.

Tonight's worksheet had four questions spread over two pages, so plenty of space to leave detailed answers. Settling back on the couch with his favorite sharpie pen, Derek got to work.

1. What is Interdependence?

> Interdependence is the universal collaborative principle that grows and develops from a sense of community and the spirit of supportive teamwork. It makes trust work, but trust still has to come first.

2. What actions and behaviors make Interdependence work and what makes it fail?

Derek began completing the T-graph Mrs. Walter's provided.

What Makes It Fail	What Makes It Work
• Trying to control everything	• Respect what people know
• Trying to think for everyone	• Appreciate what others add to the tribe/team
• Being the only leader	• Everyone takes responsibility for what they do
• Being the only ideas guy	
• Now knowing what other people are capable of	• Epowering others to do the jobs they know how to do
• Not knowing what people are naturally good at	• Rewarding collaboration

3. What is Genuineness?

Skills that help everyone be respectfully sincere, frank and forthright, and encourage kindness, respect and clear communication. It's being real all the time. It feeds into trust and interdependence.

4. What actions and behaviors make Genuineness work and what makes it fail?

Derek pondered this for a moment and filled in the details.

What Makes It Fail	What Makes It Work
• Disrespect	• Respect
• Ambivalence	• Being assertive not aggressive
• Hiding your real motives	• Being assertive and not passive
• Keeping relevant thoughts and feelings to yourself	• Learning healthy confrontation skills
• Not helping others find solutions to problems	• Honesty
	• Self-awareness
	• Learning to give clear feedback

Derek definitely wasn't the same person at work as he was at home. His wife was genuine with him anytime they needed to work on their relationship. Being two very different people, this happened often but that was okay. They wanted this relationship to work, so they were respectfully open and honest with each other. If any issues came up, they weren't afraid of making the other angry. They took a break to calm themselves and then started up again until they solved it. They took differences of opinion and misunderstandings as opportunities to strengthen their relationship and grow closer.

Unfortunately, Derek was definitely a tyrant at the office. That had never been his plan, but it had just happened. With the pressure from the people above him and all the challenges life threw at him, he never felt like he had time to deal with anyone else's problems. He was going to have to find a way to be his approachable and problem-solving real self in the face of conflict at home and at work.

This shaky eye contact and lowered gazes stuff that he'd

been noticing at work needed to stop. He made a fresh T-chart in a notebook.

Why there's no interdependence	How to create interdependence
• I tell them to do their job instead of train and help them	• I need to figure out what matters to my employees and, if they are struggling, provide corresponding training
• No one trusts anyone	
• I essentially control everything	• I need to recognize areas of cooperation and reward it when I see it
• I keep everything I'm thinking and doing to myself	
• I don't know the strengths of my employees	• I need to delegate better
	• I need to keep everyone looped in so we're on the same page

It was up to him to set the tone, to initiate the change, and lead by example. Hopefully, his actions would inspire his team to follow suit. Hopefully, being genuine about his failings as a boss would encourage them to at least try to commit to a new way of doing things. Derek drew a second T-chart.

Why I'm not genuine	How I need to be genuine
• I don't respect my coworkers	• I need to value them and tell them why
• I don't recognize what they did right	• I need to coach them and not direct them
• I'm angry all the time	• Check my emotions at the door and respond with curiosity; not criticism
• I don't listen to their problems/struggles or ideas	
• I don't know how to give good feedback	• I need to listen
• I'm afraid to fail	• Help them discover solutions by providing clear and constructive feedback
	• Let people know when they do something right

He had his work cut out for him, but the payoff would be tenfold. Everyone would be happier in a workplace where they knew their boss cared about them and was ready to help. Like Kali's tribe gathering food and supplies, Derek was sure his team would definitely start hitting deadlines and their goals if they felt safe and valued in the workplace.

He knew he was valued, or else his immediate boss, Amity, wouldn't have given him a chance to turn himself around. He'd been hired years ago because of his work skills and ambition. At first—just like his employees—he'd been great, produced great results, and even solved a technical problem the company had been struggling with for a while. He'd gotten quite a nice bonus and promotion to his new team leadership position, his current one. That's where things started unraveling. The pressure on him to keep performing distracted him from taking care of the team that existed to support him and company goals. He had done nothing in his life to develop his people skills.

Maybe it'd been a bit too much all at once and his own pride had blocked him from asking for help with his new responsibilities. However, he'd made it this far—battered and exhausted—and these universal teamwork leadership principles had lit a spark of hope. He was going to master these trust, interdependence and genuineness principles, along with the rest contained in the book.

Saturday night was just as restless, but now more principles were keeping the gears humming away inside his mind. The reasons for all the dysfunction at work were that much more clear. It was so much to learn, but he needed to learn it as fast as he could. He spent Sunday at the park with his family and did a little fishing at the duck pond. They caught a few tiny sunfish, but each fish delighted Raven all the same. Every last part of the beautiful day failed to help his mind take a break from work, the tiger book, and the principles it taught. He eagerly joined his wife and daughter for their final night of reading.

CHAPTER 9
Curiosity

Distant rumbles of thunder filled the air as the sun went down, but no rains came just yet. Lightning flashed behind the mountains, but still no rains. The bright flashes illuminated the top of a thunderhead, but it was too brief for Kali to figure out exactly which direction it was headed. Rest was going to be uneasy for everyone tonight.

Kali lay near the bridge, taking it upon himself to keep an eye on it. A handful of animals had gathered fronds and leafy branches,covering the bridge in hopes of protecting it from the rain. Several elephants and many smaller animals rested atop of the leafy bed. Hopefully, their bodies would further protect everything, holding it together.

Shadows approached from the direction of Ashoka's tribe. Kali stood when he sensed his patrolling leopards' alarm, and then grew confused when a flash of lightning showed a family of rhinos and a family of civets headed his way. He'd even caught a glimpse of sloth bears and the curved horns of water buffalo.

Were these Ashoka's animals or had Kali's former tribe members decided to return after all? He padded off on silent paws to meet the animals.

They turned out to be former tribe members and they froze when Kali stepped out of the tall grass. Kali stopped and said nothing, feeling the air for their energy as he stood beside his leopards.

"State your business," Loia, one of Kali's leopards, said.

"Ashoka has sent us to speak in private with your lord," the male rhino said. He flicked his oval-shaped ears in annoyance. "We think this is a waste of time, but he said something about this being Kali's next trial. Something about learning empathy. Your lord has made it perfectly clear that he's incapable of empathy, so this trip is clearly a waste of our time."

Flattening her ears, Loia bared her fangs and gave the rhino a warning growl.

Kali stepped forward and growled at Loia, who respectfully backed away, but continued to glare at the visitors.

"Send them away, Lord Kali," she said. "They have no respect for you."

Hardly more than a day ago, he would have agreed with her and would have chased them off. "I have not earned their respect. Let them in. I wish to hear what they have to say, along with what my brother has to teach me."

Loia looked back and forth between the visitors and her lord, and slowly the fight left her. She closed her mouth, relaxed her ears, but remained bent in a crouch. "Are you sure, Lord Kali?"

He nodded. He felt no hate or resentment; just shame for what he'd done and frustration with himself for not seeing it sooner. He could have avoided all this.

Despite the anger on her spotted face, Loia eased out of her crouch and both leopards made room to let the animals pass.

Kali said, "We're going to speak privately. Make sure no

one interrupts us." The leopards voiced their acknowledgement and the tiger lord led his former tribe members to the hillside, where his full tribe had taken refuge when the mudslide hit. The rhinos and the rest followed without a word, their hooves and paws thudding along behind him. When they reached a comfy patch of grass, Kali turned around and sat on his haunches, a gesture of invitation. The animals eyed him warily, but one rhino finally stepped forward and the civet family hopped off to hide among the water buffalo.

Aggo. That was the rhino's name. How quickly Kali had forgotten.

Aggo said, "The first thing Lord Ashoka told us to tell you is that your next trial is empathy." The rhino snorted in indignation.

"Let me start, first, by apologizing for my actions," Kali said calmly. He understood Aggo's anger. Kali had not treated any of these animals well. He needed them to trust that he was capable of listening. As a lord, that meant he had to take the first step. "My choices put every last one of you at unnecessary risk the other day. My actions over the years have made you miserable. I am aware of that now. I don't expect you to ever return to my tribe, and that's okay. All I ask of each of you is to trust that I will listen to all you have to say."

"Trust you?" a sloth bear said. "How do you expect us to trust you after all you have done?"

"I understand trusting me may be impossible for you, so tell me all I've done to create this distrust."

"You really want to know?" Aggo said, head tilted.

"Yes and no," Kali admitted. He winced at the thought of all he had done to earn such hate and distrust, but he needed to be made conscious of all his mistakes so he could avoid committing them ever again.

The rhino let out a grunt that was a disdainful laugh. "You're not going to like what you hear."

"All the more reason I need to hear it," Kali said.

The animals exchanged amused looks amongst each other. The sight made Kali clench his jaw.

"All right, then. We'll tell you everything. Brace yourself, tiger lord."

They told him everything - every last mistake, hurtful words, and demeaning actions that fostered resentment, distrust and misery. Kali had a bad habit of being hurtful and uncivil. He was always angry. Nothing anyone did was ever good enough, never done fast enough, never done exactly the way he wanted. These animals had tried so hard to please him, to earn one scrap of praise or gratitude, but had only been rewarded with anger and disdain. They could never win and felt like they could never succeed. Their efforts had slackened over the years and they had become numb to their lord's rage.

Kali held his head up just enough to establish himself as lord, but kept it lowered a bit to avoid coming off as arrogant or immune to their criticism. He really wanted to bury his head under his paws and hide from the shame. A part of him still wanted to roar at them to leave, but he held his pride at bay and listened to each animal speak their mind.

Everything they did was to appease their lord, not to achieve some common goal as a tribe. When they tried to speak up, their voices had been squashed. No one was allowed to disagree with the tiger lord. Everyone resorted to surviving and just being busy, but that didn't always lead to productivity. Their actions went from helping the tribe to trying to protect themselves from their lord's wrath. When the mudslide had nearly cost everyone their lives, it had been the last straw for the animals standing before him.

After the last animal spoke, they all fell quiet. Lightning and thunder were still distant and intermittent, but a cold wind carrying the smell of rain chilled them. It was a sign that the storm was getting closer.

Kali pushed aside thoughts of the storm as his former tribe

members' words bounced around in his head like predators fighting over a meal. He had committed so many wrongs, far more than he realized. His chest rose and fell with a deep sigh. This was a lot to absorb. He kept his gaze lowered out of respect. "Thank you for your honesty. A genuine apology cannot fix all I've done. I will take all you've said into consideration so I may become a better lord for those still under my care."

"You really have changed," Aggo said in disbelief. "I would not have believed it had I not come. What brought about this change?"

Kali allowed himself a small smile. "You have a good lord who is also a good brother to me. I do apologize for all the wrongs I have done to each of you. Even though my actions were intended for the good of the tribe and to protect it, I now see that I was a bigger threat than the mudslide. I do understand why you feel the way you do. If I were in your paws, I would probably feel similar. It makes sense. You make sense."

Aggo nodded agreement, but said nothing. They had already said what they needed to say.

"I will think long on all of this for the sake of my tribe." Kali met their gazes at last. He was met with open surprise and many of them looked quite pleased, grateful that he had made good on his promise to listen. Even if none of them ever came back, he found solace in what he saw and felt in this moment. It was enough to allow him to move forward. "Now, what did my brother say about this empathy trial?"

The animals all looked to Aggo, who said, "Lord Ashoka has instructed you to build empathy with your tribe. It is a valuable tool for building a strong tribe that knows how to trust one another and work together. It fosters kindness, happiness, and an ability to listen to and understand one another. Whether you agree or not, it makes everyone feel valued. He said empathy is crucial when it comes to getting a tribe to work together - and for resolving misunderstandings and conflict. A tribe is most unified when empathy is strong. Each member is curious and filled with a desire to understand another animal whether they agree or not. It builds a desire to be the best an animal can be, to always grow and learn, and to be conscious of how your own actions affect others and not just yourself."

"Thank you. I will ponder on this as well." He stood. "Now, real quickly before you go, may I ask if your bridge is done?"

"It is."

"Are you moving it into place tonight or tomorrow?"

"We are waiting to see if the rains are bad. We have already weighed the consequences of putting off the moving of the bridge and have decided it's best to take action when we have more energy to act."

Kali nodded thoughtfully. "I have much to think on. My leopards will see you safely to the river. Good night and good luck."

"Good night, Lord Kali," the animals said.

A young civet bounded up to Kali. It was barely bigger than his paw, but it wrapped its little arms and striped tail around his leg and hugged tight. Kali smiled, warmed by the gesture. He gently licked the civet on the forehead, garnering a delighted giggle, and it bounded back to its family.

The first drops of rain sprinkled the ground and the wind picked up a little as his former tribe members departed. Hopefully, the storm would allow him enough time to learn empathy before it arrived in full force. The raindrops were cold, a sign of a strong storm.

CHAPTER 10
Forgiveness

Intermittent raindrops sprinkled his back as he approached the mound of animals lying or sitting on the bridge. His pace slowed at the sound of low, somber voices, and he stopped altogether when he heard the gibbons talking about the home they'd lost.

"What if this new jungle is dangerous?" Rekhan's little daughter said in a timid voice. "What if the trees aren't as comfy to sleep in?"

Rekhan rubbed his daughter's back and occasionally plucked something from her fur. "The predators will protect us and the trees will be comfy. You will see."

"But I miss home. Why did we stop digging?"

The gibbon's furry frame rose and fell with a resigned sigh. "The trees that fell will never stand up again. We cannot wait for new ones to grow. That will take too long. The new trees will be just as good. I promise."

"But it won't be the same."

"No. It won't." Rekhan kissed the top of his daughter's head. "But that's okay. Change is a part of life, little one. Change is often scary, but good can come out of it if you're willing to see the advantages and move through it. Our new home in new trees will be safer. We won't be on the side of a mountain and in danger of another mudslide. We will be much less likely to lose our home like this again."

The daughter curled up in Rekhan's lap and clutched his sides. "I will. But I still wish we didn't have to move."

He held her tight. "Me, too."

A sloth bear next to them rolled over so he could see the gibbons. "Same here, little one. Moving is a lot of work and none of us know what to expect in this new place, but we will make it home and do everything we can to make it good."

His pawsteps masked by the light patter of rain, Kali stepped out of the tall grass and into view of animals camped on the bridge. Animals turned at his arrival, including Rekhan and his family. Kali padded over to the gibbons. "I will miss this home, too," he said softly. And it was true. He had picked this piece of land for its location. It was near a steady water supply, lined on one side by a ravine that offered protection, and it was right next to the jungle for hunting and grazing. There had been nothing but an open field before he'd gathered animals to him. They'd built the village from scratch. It had taken years to make it what is was, yet it had taken no more than one night to wipe it all away.

Despite the flaws, failures, and dysfunction, he would still miss it.

"I didn't realize I wasn't the only one who'd miss it. I thought you'd all be happy to get away from a place full of so many bad memories."

The elephant named Habba said, "There is that, but this place is also where many of us met our mates and started families. We have made friendships and shared our lives here, too."

"That is good to hear," Kali said, the guilt in his chest loosening its grip a little. "I know you all need rest, but I had a long conversation with former tribe members that has left me with a few questions for the rest of you - if you have the energy."

"Lord Kali, you look exhausted," the sloth bear said.

"It was a difficult conversation, but I am grateful for it. I have learned much." Kali told them all he had discovered. His tribe listened intently, some of the farther ones coming closer. Their lord invited them to make him aware of where else he had been unfair and cruel. "I want to be a great lord, the best lord you could ask for. I need to know, so I can learn and change for the better. I want this to be the best tribe in the jungle."

A thoughtful silence followed, which produced a few shrugs. Habba raised her trunk a little as a sign of respect. "All is forgiven, Lord Kali. We will hold you to your word about becoming the best lord. I promise to acknowledge your successes, and make you aware of your mistakes as they happen. I promise to help you become great."

"As do I," Rekhan said.

"And so do I," the sloth bear said.

More and more animals voiced their agreement until it had rippled through the entire tribe. Kali's heart rose with each voice, each promise, and his eyes stung with heartfelt gratitude. He inclined his head to them. "Thank you. Very much. Now everyone get some rest."

His tribe tucked themselves in, packing together on and around the bridge, and heads disappeared among paws and flanks. His tribe looked like a furry, leathery mound that rose and fell with their breath. A lazy rain rolled in as thunder and lightning continued to interrupt the night. Kali tried to settle down, but he was restless and night was his prime waking time. Instead, he joined his leopards and panthers in patrolling their soon-to-be former territory. They encountered nothing threatening, most likely due to the storm. Hunting in the rain was great cover when trying to prowl unheard. Hunting in a storm was dangerous due to the lightning and wind, the flashes making it hard to see. Their eyes had to constantly readjust to the fluctuation between light and dark.

Over the course of the night the storm moved on, but the rains stayed and grew steadier. The clogged river grew and spread but, thankfully, Kali and his tribe had thought to build the bridge far enough away from the river to keep it out of immediate danger. In the morning, the tribe woke slowly after a night of poor sleep and two days of hard labor. No one made a complaint as they fed and watered themselves before gathering around the bridge. Kali stood atop it. Moving the bridge into place was going to be dangerous no matter how they approached the task.

Before Kali could call his animals back to the bridge, Ashoka arrived once more, this time without Kali's leopard's escorting him. They had finally started to trust the visiting tiger lord. Kali trotted out to meet him.

The brothers butted heads in greeting and Ashoka said, "Your bridge looks amazing. You and your tribe have done very well. I'm proud of all of you."

"Much credit goes to you for helping me become a better lord," Kali said humbly.

Ashoka shrugged. "You're the one who committed to change. How are you healing, by the way?"

"Better. I am sore, but I can move." The long patrol had loosened him up. Now he just ached from the battering he took, both physical and verbal. "I am well on the mend."

His brother nodded thoughtfully. "That is good."

"What is today's trial?"

Ashoka smiled. "Today, I give you your last two trials: risk and success. The last one, success, is strongly tied to the other five trials. I wish to explain risk and success to you and your tribe before you move your bridge. While you could all just use our bridge should your's fail, I would rather you all experience the success of being able to cross your own bridge. You have come too far just to lose all your hard work to the ravine."

The thought of losing his bridge at the last moment made Kali's stomach turn. That would be crushing to everyone. All that hard work would be for nothing. They had to do it and think of everything they could to avoid failure.

"Risk is a part of any task," said Ashoka. "We run the risk of getting injured or suffering from a failed attempt every time we hunt, but the reward is food. Our fishers take risks every time they venture into dangerous waters with crocodiles and pythons, but the reward is meals for many. Our job as lords is to pick the right animals that are best suited to reason through and minimize certain risks. We teach them what we already know. Then we help them become better by using honest mistakes in learning stories that we tell others so they don't repeat those mistakes. Next we teach them how to solve problems and make decisions. We are all responsible for remembering how we solved problems and corrected mistakes. But we can't just sit on a log afraid to move forward or backward while we ponder the risk we are taking. We must take action."

"That makes sense," Kali said. "No lord can possibly juggle every last risk a tribe faces at any given moment. And, when it is time to change, we have to move forward." Even though he had tried to succeed over the years, he recognized his own fear of failure had often got in the way. All he'd done was make himself and the rest of the tribe miserable. "So in order to properly manage risk, I must trust?"

Ashoka smiled again. "Correct. Each trial I've given you is intertwined with the other five. Trust is the foundation that makes way for interdependence, being genuine, practicing empathy, assessing risk, and, finally, creating success, both individually and as a tribe."

Kali thought about how instilling trust in his tribe had made it possible to get the bridge built. Trust placed him in the position to listen and build empathy and safety for genuineness to emerge. This resulted in a trustworthy tribe that cooperated with one another. Despite the circumstances, they were all much happier. Now they had successfully built a bridge without going hungry or thirsty, and without getting attacked by rogue predators. All this contributed to a long list of successes, both individually and tribe-wide, and everything fueled their bridge-building process. "I see. The tribe has become unified under our shared goal of getting a bridge built."

"Correct. Are you beginning to see the tiger in each tribe member? Do you see that they are trustworthy, interdependent, genuine, empathetic, risk-resolving and successful? Doesn't it feel different to behave this way?"

Kali did see it. At first, he hadn't wanted to. He had wanted to be the only tiger, which was more a matter of his own self-esteem and worth, rather than seeing a tiger lord in others. But, the more Kali illuminated his tribe's full potential, the more grateful he felt each of them was more like a tiger than he thought. "They have grown loyal and ambitious. Each of them contributes to the tribe to the best of their ability and in their own way. They all have a winning fierceness to them. And we are all much happier. I must admit they are all tigers at least in spirit."

"Indeed they are," Ashoka said proudly. "We are going to need every last drop of fierceness getting our bridges into place. Ours is of similar size and shape, and equally heavy-looking. Do you have any idea how you're going to move yours?"

Kali turned to the bridge. A team of macaques, gibbons, elephants and civets examined the bridge from end to end, testing the mud and sap to see how much had been washed away, how well the vines held, and if any trees showed signs of rot. The ground was wet, muddy and slick once more. While the storm had not directly hit them, it was enough to make this next task even more challenging. "Not yet."

"We have discussed it over the past couple of days, but the

real planning is happening right now." Ashoka looked at the ravine. "I wish you had an easier task to learn the ins and outs of risk. There really isn't any room for failure on this one."

Kali's chest rose and fell with a sigh. "No, but we are ready. We will do this."

Ashoka studied the bridge in silence a moment longer before turning back to his brother. "My tribe has an elder gibbon, named Anja, with an impeccable memory. She has only one working eye, but the running joke is that she has three eyes that see everything - even what others are thinking," he said with a smile. "Anyway, she has been watching everything, making mental notes of every step and procedure. Anja knows how many trees it took, how many animals to gather them, how to lay and lash them together, how much sap we used, how long this all took, and so on. Should we ever need another bridge in a new place, we will have a story passed down through generations with all the details recorded in it."

"I wish I'd thought of that," Kali said. It would have come in handy if the storm had ruined the bridge. Gauging by the silence of the animals surrounding the bridge, they had found nothing concerning.

"It is something to consider. That new bit of jungle looks good, but who knows what the future holds? Now our tribe knows we can build another bridge, should the need arise." Ashoka faced the ravine, the tip of his tail lazily twitching back and forth. "I can't tell you the best way to place a bridge over a ravine. We have never attempted something like this before. All I can say is give them your trust again. Don't act on a plan until you're wholly confident in it—or at least as confident as possible. If you are confident in their ideas, they will be confident when they act. If any steps sounded good along the way, but new and unforeseen circumstances show they are not, step in for the sake of everyone's safety."

"I will."

"I know you can do this, brother. I know your tribe can."

Kali smiled. "See you on the other side, then." His brother smiled back, nodded, and took off at a fast trot toward his tribe and bridge. Kali returned to his own bridge and called everyone to him with a roar.

***

With his entire tribe before him, Lord Kali said, "Before we start moving the bridge, we must discuss how to best get this done, like we did with building the bridge. The challenge with this task is that the risk is much higher than squished fingers and trampled tails. Not only will we be in danger of falling into the ravine, we could drop the bridge into it. We need a plan that minimizes the risk for everyone and everything involved. To do that, we are going to revisit how we built our action plan for the bridge. I want you all to choose a group of animals, whom you trust are the best thinkers and strategizers, to get this bridge in place. I will work with those animals to form an action plan, and then we will get to work. Also, send me the animal you all believe has the best memory in the tribe."

The tribe drew into a circle and began talking amongst each other, letting everyone take their turn. There was minimal talking over each other with everyone making an effort to be polite and listen. A few animals kept trying to interject, but other animals gave warning growls or gently swatted at them. Kali patrolled the outside, listening to every word and marveling at their teamwork. They were all so eager to work together and be respectful, including the ones that had to be reeled in. There was trust connecting them that must have been there all this time, buried under Kali's tyranny, but it had resurfaced literally overnight, as if it had never disappeared.

After some time, an eclectic mix of animals met with Kali atop the bridge. There was even a frog and cobra among the elephants, water buffalo, simians and birds, and they all stood together, the smaller animals perched on the larger ones.

Kali stood before them proudly. "All right, let's figure out how to safely move a bridge."

Despite having just a dozen animals to strategize the most dangerous part of their goal to get safely across the ravine, it took hours to talk it out. After the first hour, Kali was worried he was doing something wrong, but one look at Ashoka's tribe and their bridge still lay inert, too. Kali's select animals kept finding holes in plans, details that unraveled ideas everyone originally liked, and more details cropped up as the length of the conversation grew. They all talked animatedly, eagerly. Not one of them gave the slightest inkling they were afraid of sharing ideas with their lord and each other. The conversation was open and respectful. With no one afraid to share their ideas and concerns, everyone was able to look at ideas and strategies from every angle.

Each animal had a way of looking at problems and figuring out how to solve them. And with all these different perspectives, they were able to look at this bridge task from multiple angles, solve all the problems they faced, and minimize the risk. There was no way to completely eliminate the danger part, unless they gave up on their goal, but that was out of the question. Even crossing Ashoka's bridge instead was out of the question. They took great pride in their bridge. They were going to see this to the end and do everything they could to succeed. Their commitment made Kali proud. He could almost see the stripes in their hides and fur. He ruled a tribe full of trustworthy, interdependent, genuine, empathetic, risk resolving and successful tigers, for sure.

A solid plan formed in due time. A younger macaque named Yadai listened to the whole thing. She was the animal the entire tribe believed had the best memory of all of them. Kali tested her memory with a few obscure questions about her experience in the tribe and her life, and she was able to answer all of them quickly and thoroughly. She remembered the names of all the tribe members who'd left, precisely how many had left, the kingfisher that was lazy at providing fish for the tribe, and the name of Kali's mother, which was Shira.

Yadai had been a wiggly little thing while listening to the plan unfold, scurrying between legs, hanging from tusks and horns, but her ears had always been pricked in the direction of who spoke. At one point, she even politely mentioned that they'd already talked about how to push the bridge into place and quickly went over the steps. From there, she scurried atop Habba's head and started grooming the elephant. After a moment of surprise from the rest of the circle, the animals resumed planning.

A few times through the conversation—since it was getting so long and detailed—they asked Yadai to summarize parts and repeat steps in the process, which she did perfectly. Hearing pieces repeated to them helped them hear how the plan sounded. They spotted steps that needed more planning and addressed these details as well.

By the time Kali, Yadai and the rest of the group agreed they had the soundest plan possible, they were all ready for a nap. That was so much thinking. They yawned and stretched out their legs and wings, getting the blood flowing again, and then returned to the rest of the tribe. Food, vines and more fallen trees had been gathered.

Kali hopped atop the bridge and faced his tribe. This was it. This was the moment they'd all been eagerly anticipating and dreading. Their trust, interdependence, genuineness, empathy, risk resolution and success was going to be put to the test. They were eager to succeed, but also afraid of failing, even Kali. But, there was no log sitting—none at all.

When Kali felt afraid, he remembered a question his mother once asked him—a question that had once been asked of her, too: What would you do if you weren't afraid? Kali didn't know who was the first to ask that, but he knew he'd tackle this final trial with maximum effort if he weren't afraid. Somehow having a well thought-through action plan always robbed fear of its hold over him. He stood proudly before his tribe. "We have a good, strong plan. This is what we're going to do…"

CHAPTER 11
Testing New Bridges

Every last bird, predator and grazer gathered among the vines and dug in their claws, held in their beaks, or wrapped their talons around the first vine. Kali gave them a countdown and, as one, they began flapping. The vine rose off the ground and the concerted wing flapping created a gust that filled their ears with the thudding wing beats. Snakes and colorful frogs marked where to place each end of the vine (some frogs had been flown to the other side already) and a pair of crested hawk-eagles monitored everything from above.

The first vine was placed across the ravine and the bigger, stronger birds gathered at each end to hold it tight as macaques scurried across with another vine slung over their shoulders. They moved swiftly and confidently, their tails loosely wrapped around the first vine in case they slipped. They all knew to drop the vine if just one of them slipped.

The macaques placed the second vine without incident and an elephant held onto one end of the vines while the macaques and birds held onto the other. With a third vine clamped in his toes, a gibbon moved hand-over-hand across the vines as quickly as he could and made it to the other side. A second gibbon followed with a fourth vine, coiling it around the other three has he went, and then took over holding the vine for all the other animals. Birds and macaques returned to the rest of the tribe while an eagle guided the first gibbon to some rocks and smaller trees that would be used to hold the first bunch of vines in place. There were no large trees close to the ravine, so they had to create something to tie the vines to.

The whole process was repeated with a second set of vines at the frog-marked location and more gibbons crossed the ravine to help gather rocks and small trees. A squad of thirty gibbons made their way across, carefully pulling behind them yet more vines.

Gibbons and macaques on the far side of the ravine worked together to wrap the lead vines around a small tree, and then proceeded to a second small tree, binding them together with a few twists to secure them before plunging them into the ground and securing them with rocks. More gibbons and macaques on Kali's side of the ravine tied the bridge vines to Habba's tusks.

The simians used their combined strength to hold the vines securely as four leopards straddled the vines with front legs hanging over one set, and back legs hanging over the other.

Just like they'd practiced, Habba started walking backwards. The vines grew taut. She raised her head, creating a slope with the drooping vines, and the leopards began sliding along them. Loia, the youngest of the leopards, started giggling and found the whole thing fun, even with a deadly drop below them. The other leopards dangled with stiff limbs as they all slid to the far side of the ravine. The tribe let out a collective sigh of relief and a few cheered as the leopards clawed their way onto flat ground one at a time. The older leopards shook themselves as Loia let out a triumphant growl.

The gibbons and macaques worked together to strengthen the two trees and the vines wrapped around them on the far side of the ravine. The leopards leaned into the trees with their chests, holding them upright while gibbons pulled the vines tight. The simians then grabbed the vines attached to Habba and all the animals braced themselves as the first blue bull straddled the vines as the leopards had. The beast slid along the vines to the other side of the ravine, and nine more beasts followed. Now there was a pulling team on the other side of the ravine that was strong enough to pull the bridge across.

So far, so good, but still far from done!

Since the bridge had been built a modest distance from the ravine, the vines didn't reach the bridge yet. A pair of elephants held onto the waiting vines while the rest of the elephants and water buffalo lined up alongside the bridge. Kali positioned himself at the forefront, gave them a countdown, and let out a roar to signal them to lift the structure as one. Muscles bulged in unison and the bridge rose off the ground, riding on tusks and horns, but it rose unevenly and a few animals slipped.

Kali roared again. "Hold on. Put it down. I'm going to move a few of you." While they probably could move the bridge with the current lineup, the tiger lord didn't want to take any risks. His animals set the bridge down with a thud strong enough only to make the ground vibrate. A few onlookers watched in alarm, but the bridge only let out a small creak of protest. Kali reorganized a few elephants and water buffalo to even out their strength, and returned to the head of the bridge. They had originally agreed to evenly spacing the elephants among the water buffalo, but the first lift had shown that some buffalo were stronger than they had originally thought.

The second lift was much more even. It wasn't perfect, but it was near enough to satisfy Kali. With the help of birds and the frogs, he guided the bridge to the vines with one slow, careful step at a time. Carriers slipped now and then, and a couple times

Kali had to remind them to move slowly. The slipping spiked their adrenaline and quickened their pace, but they had to do this carefully. When discussing this step, Kali and his think tank had agreed that slow and steady was far safer than rushing it. If they rushed, they ran the risk of tripping over one another, getting trampled and, at worst, getting crushed by a dropped bridge.

The animals keeping a steady pace outnumbered the ones who panicked. Snorts and heavy breathing filled the air as the bridge approached the ravine. With the help of eagles, Kali guided the bridge to rest between the rows of frogs. He inadvertently backed into the rhino guarding the ravine edge and Kali experienced a moment of terror as he realized how close he'd come to blindly falling to his doom. Thankfully, they'd had the foresight to place an animal there to prevent just that.

The bridge was dropped into place and Kali's heart rate settled as the carriers caught their breath.

"Great job, all of you," Kali said. "The bridge is exactly where we need it to be."

The two vine tying teams swooped in and set to work attaching the vines to the bridge. The last trunk, laid parallel to the ravine, purposely had a gap between it and the next trunk. Vines were woven in and out of the gap, pulled tight, and tied, creating two great, corded arms stretching across the ravine. They were ready to pull the bridge into place.

Two elephants, a fresh team of buffalo, and the adult rhinos gathered around the bridge. Kali trotted over to the animals and took a deep breath. "On my signal!" He counted down in a loud voice and let out a mighty roar. The animals pushed and lifted and the bridge lurched forward before coming to a stop. Hooves and rounded feet stomped in the mud as they worked together to line the bridge back up. Kali counted down and bellowed another roar. The bridge lurched forward again and the leading edge jutted out over the ravine. The onlookers gathered at the ravine and every bird took to the sky. How so many birds could fly so closely without knocking each other out of the sky, he'd never know, but he set the thought aside as he timed another roar. The bridge lurched again.

The pulling team on the other side of the ravine dug hooves and claws into the ground with every roar and drove the two small trees and trunks closer to the new patch of jungle. Macaques and gibbons hooted and hollered encouragement.

The onlookers on the ground cheered the movers, and the birds screeched and cawed their excitement. Once the bridge was halfway across, they switched the pushing teams and went back at it. Excitement grew as the gap closed one push at a time. Onlookers crowded closer and closer, until the leopards ordered them back. Another detail they'd thought of was making sure everyone else kept a safe distance while the movers worked on the bridge. If any of the vines broke, they had no way of knowing how the bridge would move. It might just dive into the ravine, or it might swing around before falling, possibly taking an animal or two with it. Sloth bears helped the leopards keep the rest of the tribe back, but the bears tolerated smaller animals watching the progress from atop their furry backs.

The leading edge of the bridge rammed into the far end of the ravine on the next push, causing all the elephants and buffalo to stumble, the bridge let out a teeth-clenching groan, and the gibbon group scrambled to the ravine. The bridge had been sinking a little lower with each push. The eagles had warned them of this. They'd removed a handful of buffalo to reduce the might, but the bridge moved with more ease than anticipated. Now, the back end was raised a few paws off the ground while the leading edge sat wedged a few paws below the lip of the ravine. They all stopped and stared.

It took a long moment, but Kali's brain finally started working again as he realized the bridge wasn't about to fall. "Yadai," he said, his voice echoing off the rock. The energetic macaque scurried over and crouched before him.

"Yes, Lord Kali?"

"What was our plan if something like this happened?" They'd talked for so long about so many details that his brain drew a blank.

Yadai tilted her head. "We didn't think of this precise scenario. We anticipated the bridge sinking a little, but not ramming into the other end." She hopped onto the bridge, raising herself above Kali's head. "What if you had the elephants carefully step on this end while the blue bulls lift on their end?"

"What if we pull it backwards a little, and then try again?" Habba said.

"That might work, too," Yadai said agreeably.

Kali thought a moment. "Let's discuss this. We're so close. Let's not rush."

The discussion lasted long enough to weigh all their options, the pros and cons of each choice, and soon they were able to commit as a group to the next course of action. Eagles flew over and informed the pulling team of the plan. Once two groups of gibbons and bulls each returned with another small tree trunk, two elephants on Kali's side got into place at the raised end of the bridge.

At Kali's word, the elephants began pulling. The bridge didn't budge so he ordered two more elephants join in. The beasts grunted and wood and vines groaned. Right as Kali called over two more elephants, the bridge finally jerked free of the other end of the ravine. Animals and birds cheered and screeched in triumph. Gibbons jammed trees between bridge and ledge, and bulls pulled down on the vines tied to their short horns. The two waiting elephants rose onto their hind legs and it was like watching mountains rear up. They were huge compared to a tiger. Rounded feet came down on the bridge. One by one, the other elephants added their feet to the bridge. Their combined efforts created enough leverage to even the bridge out. The pulling team on the other side split themselves between holding the trees in place and pulling on the vines tied to the bridge. The team of water buffalo lowered their heads and pushed on the bridge. Elephants removed their feet from the bridge at the last moment and the structure lurched. This time, the leading edge slid atop the other side, scattering the gibbons and leopards. The elephants helped with one last push, and the bridge was in place at last.

Animals cheered. They'd done it! Kali opened his mouth to roar with them, but a chunk of rock directly under the other side of the bridge broke off and fell into the ravine. The excitement died as everyone watched the rock drop silently out of sight.

They had constructed the bridge to overlap each side of the ravine by the length of an adult elephant. There was still plenty of ground supporting that end of the bridge, but would more rock break away if they tried using the bridge?

Eyes still on the ravine, Kali turned to his tribe. "Stay here. I'll go first."

"No, Lord Kali!" one of the water buffaloes said, eyes wide with terror. "What if more rock breaks away?"

He hopped onto the edge of the bridge. "Then you will know not to follow me. My brother is a good lord. He will take good care of you should the worst happen."

"Please don't do this," Yadai said, touching Kali's rear paw. "It's not worth the risk. We built the bridge. We got it in place. That's enough. We can use Lord Ashoka's."

Kali shook his head. "This is something I must do. Now, stay here."

Yadai whimpered, but said nothing.

Scanning his tribe, Kali took in each of their worried faces, and then began to cross the bridge.

The wood felt solid under his paws, and the width of the bridge was wide enough to keep him from feeling dizzy with so much open air under him. Crossing the bridge felt similar to sitting high up in a tree. The height didn't bother him. It was not knowing if the rock would hold that made his heart pound like a stampeding horde of buffalo in his chest. If anyone shouted anything, he couldn't hear it over the thudding in his ears.

Kali made it to the other end and his gibbons, blue bulls and leopards stared at him in open amazement.

"It held," one of them said in breathy awe.

"It did," Kali said and crossed the bridge once more, this time at a trot. It was more than stable enough to handle a tiger, but what about their biggest tribe members? "Habba, do you have the courage to cross?"

The elephant stepped forward. "You don't have to ask me twice." She followed Kali across and the wood made no complaint about the extra load. His sensitive ears didn't pick up the slightest sound of cracking rock and not a single pebble broke away. Habba safely stepped onto the awaiting grass and turned around. "It held," she said with equal awe.

Kali smiled and returned to the rest of the tribe once more. They gathered at the edge of the bridge. "Congratulations. You have built a strong bridge. You have all done very well. Now, come. Let's pick a new home."

Kali led his tribe of "tigers" across the bridge and into the nice jungle waiting to be their new home.

CHAPTER 12
Hopes and Ideas

"The end," Derek Alexander said. He looked at his daughter, expecting her to start applauding, but she lay fast asleep with a faint smile on her face. Closing the book, he smiled.

"Whatcha think?" Martha said softly and kissed Raven on the forehead. Their daughter remained sound asleep.

"I thought it was amazing," he said, also softly. They carefully slide out from under the unicorn comforter. Derek waved for his wife to follow and together they returned to the kitchen. Feeling wide awake for the first time in a while, he grabbed a notebook and pencil from a drawer, and joined Martha at the table. He set the book in the middle and opened the notebook to a fresh page.

"I got so much out of the story," Derek said. "I think I know how to fix the office nightmare caused by my leadership." He was about to jot something down when he noticed the word "TIGERS" written vertically in all capital letters. Stemming off each letter was a full word: Trust, Interdependence, Genuineness,

Empathy, Risk, Success. TIGERS. The six trials. He let out a thoughtful "huh." He looked at his wife. "It's sort of bad, because this means I'm the real problem at the office. We're losing people and falling farther and farther behind because of me."

"I've seen you take notes these past two nights. Care to let me in on them?"

Derek grimaced. "I'm angry and I micromanage all the time like Kali. Look at these trials here, these principles." He pointed to the back cover and read the six words aloud. "I don't trust my employees and they probably don't trust me back. It makes so much sense now. It took Kali some time to earn it back and he had help along the way. I'd be lucky if anyone would be willing to help me become a better manager."

"Is there anyone in the office the employees really like and look up to?"

"There is," he said slowly, remembering Catherine, a fellow project manager he'd always thought was on a mission to make him look bad. Her team loved her, was super efficient, and produced great work. Derek had tried borrowing employees, on occasion, in hopes of fixing his team, but they'd all left him within days and returned to their assigned manager. After the first two left in a huff, Catherine had tried talking to him about what she'd heard, but he'd shot her down and accused her of having less-than-noble intentions. He grimaced at the memory. "I owe her a big apology though."

"No time like the present, then."

"Do you think she'll forgive me?" He hadn't used professional words when telling her to leave his office. She had every right to shut him out if he tried to approach her.

"If she's as good a manager as you think she is, then probably."

Derek let out a slow sigh. "Here's to hoping. I guess this is one place where trust comes into play, too." He looked at the lined page in the notebook. "This book's story runs such a perfect parallel to what's going on at the office that it's eerie. We've been hit by an emotional storm and a mudslide of failures has ground everything to a halt. If I don't make some critical changes, we're going to fall in the proverbial ravine. I could put all of us out of jobs and the CEO would just find another team to replace us." Now that he thought about it, this wasn't just about his job. The future of his team's jobs were at stake, too.

Martha looked slightly startled by this comment.

"I'm sorry to scare you, but it probably is that bad. And, like Kali, it's probably all my fault." He sank into his chair, humility roiling around in his chest. So much fell into place when he applied those six principles to himself.

Gentle hands touched his arm, resting on his forearm. "It takes great courage and humility to acknowledge such truths. As my husband, I don't want to believe that you are the cause of the dysfunction, but if you believe it then how do you want to fix it?"

Derek placed a hand on top of hers. "Did you ever have a hard time trusting any of your employees?"

A small smile touched her mouth. "Oh, yes. Going from doing everything yourself to delegating the work is challenging. I want everything done perfectly, but the reality is that I can't do everything. I have to trust the people I hire to commit to my principles and goals, and do everything they can to excel at their jobs and help the company grow. It's a mystery at first with each new employee, but I give each of them a chance to show me how committed and genuine they are. I've been fortunate to hire a handful of good people and only let go one person who turned out to be just in it for the paycheck."

"I'm sorry that they disappointed you."

Martha squeezed his arm. "It's okay. The rest of my employees were so much happier when I let that one go. He was dragging everyone down. But anyway, yes, it takes a leap of faith to give employees a chance to validate your trust. Most will meet you halfway. The rest simply aren't a good fit. It's nothing personal." She looked up at him. "And that part is important to remember. Whenever you have to let someone go, it's because their behavior and skill set is better suited elsewhere. If the person you're letting go wants to take it personally, that's on them. And, it is usually after you have had many conversations already anyway."

"Makes sense," Derek said thoughtfully. He wrote the word "trust" in all-capitals on the first line and jotted a few notes. "I may take this book into work with me tomorrow. There are so many good things to learn from it, both as managers and employees."

"Catherine might like it, too."

"Good idea!" This might help prove to her that he was serious about becoming a better manager, and maybe even convince her to forgive and help him. "I need help repairing trust. I need her to be my Ashoka. Since I've done so much damage already, I think I need a person like her to share some insights that help me repair everything."

"I like that idea," Martha said. "I have a feeling she'll be happy to help. You're part of the same company and have the same ultimate goals. You both just have different jobs that support the company in your own ways."

Derek agreed. "So *trust* will be the first thing to tackle. No one at any level will agree to work with me on any other principle until I earn at least some trust back. So that means *interdependence* is second." He jotted the word and a few notes down. "I realize now that I need to stop micromanaging my staff and just let them do their job. That's why they try so hard after they're first hired, and then slowly give up as time passes." He scribbled down some more notes, excited at the thought of so many things going smoother just by leaving his employees alone and being available if they needed help. All he really needed to do was comment on what they are doing right and check in to see if they hit any snags. Kali's tribe had functioned so much smoother once he'd been forced to sit back and let them do their jobs. Derek was so used to bouncing from person to person and meddling with their work. It was going to take a huge effort on his part to stop that. Still, he wouldn't miss everyone getting stressed and tensed at the sight of him. Instead of getting angry with them for the reaction, he would be understanding and seek to understand what they were going through—listening to them and learning how he could use his power to remove an obstacle rather than micro-manage. His actions had caused so much tension in the office.

The next word was *genuineness*. He jotted that down. "I've definitely been nothing but a genuine pain all this time. Do you think I should talk to all of them one-on-one, like Kali did?"

"If you want to be genuine in your efforts to fix all this, then yes," Martha said patiently. "Each of them will have taken your words and actions in their own way, and internalized them differently. Plus, they'll appreciate the one-on-one, especially if you can get them to speak their mind. It's really freeing to be able to let your genuine self shine in the workplace, instead of feeling like you have to take on a different personality to survive. It gets exhausting to pretend to be someone else eight hours a day."

"Do you pretend to be someone else, too?"

Derek rubbed his face with both hands. "Yes," he said between his wrists. "I don't yell at you or Raven - or boss you around. I don't even micromanage you two, either."

"I meant more personality-wise. How are you at patience and personability and whatnot compared to at home?"

He lowered his hands. "I don't have any patience at the office. I'm not kind or personable. I don't talk about sports or music or anything fun with anyone. It's all work, work, work. I don't know anything about anyone beyond how much coffee and energy drinks people guzzle every day. I don't even know what kind of coffee they like."

Derek nodded. "I will have to work on being genuine, too. I'd rather people smile when they see me, instead of grimacing. I need to let them see that I am human, too, and that I want them to be human around me. Their fear of me and my anger with them has created a vicious cycle. That stops tomorrow." He made a few more notes before writing *empathy* on the next page. "I think I learned empathy while reading this book. My team has been trying so hard to appease my temper, instead of contributing to the team goal. They're all just trying to survive until they either quit or get fired. We can't go on like this. We're never going to succeed until we're all on the same page and working together. This means I must listen in order to understand what they are thinking and feeling, despite what I think is right."

Empathy, if Derek understood it correctly, was seeking to understand someone whether they agreed or not. It requires good listening, not reacting, and asking good questions so that he could understand. Then, once he understood his employee, he could contribute to solutions from a point of collaboration in order to help them both get what they needed! His team had to be willing to stand up for what they needed rather than just accommodating his temper, which meant there had to be a safe process for even the meek ones.

Martha planted a kiss on his cheek. "I'm so pleased you got as much out of the book as you did. I want you to succeed and be happy."

"For how long did you have an inkling my leadership skills were suffering?"

His wife sat quietly a moment studying his notebook. "Awhile now. I was unsure of whether or not I should say anything. I also didn't know how you'd take it."

"Looks like I need to make sure I have a tiger for a wife, too. I don't want you to be afraid of being genuine or honest with me. I want to be the husband you deserve. I want this to be a happy, safe home for all of us."

"Thank you, honey," she said as she leaned in for a kiss. "You already are. I look forward to growing wiser and older together."

"Same." He set the worksheet on the last three trials/principles and skipped straight to the empathy T-chart. He would get to the preceding questions later.

What Makes Empathy Work	What Makes It Fail
• Concern for emotional safety and needs of others • Listening to others with curiosity and the desire to understand • Healthy boundaries • Being a mentor/coach • Being aware of what I am feeling	• Selfishness • Not meeting human needs at the workplace • Ignoring other people's feelings • Being a dictator • Creating stiff competition between co-workers for rewards and recognition

Derek was sure there was more to it, but these points were the most obvious to him, and with those bullet points in mind, he made another T-chart on the back of the worksheet.

Why I'm not empathetic	How I need to be empathetic
• Ignoring how everyone feels and what they think	• Understand how my actions have made people feel
• Caring about the bottom line more than people doing the work	• Being curious and not judgmental
• I never listen	• Listen with the goal to understand
• I boss and micromanage because I don't want to fail	• Being more aware of my own knee-jerk reactions

Derek wrote down *risk* but didn't add any notes. He wasn't sure what to put yet. Perhaps he wouldn't be sure until tomorrow, but then he remembered the part in the story where the Kali and Ashoka had spoken before they both worked on moving their bridges. "When it comes to risk, I think I have a lot of good people working under me. They've been trained and everything. I think I need to change how I handle and view mistakes, both mine and theirs. I have to see mistakes for the learning opportunities they are. My employees are not perfect. I'm not perfect. I need to stop trying to squeeze perfection out of each of them and instead help them grow." He looked at his wife. "We've grown as a couple, learned things together, but the difference is we've always been eager to work together. We don't give up on our marriage when things weren't perfect. I need to start treating the office the same way."

Smiling, Martha nodded. "Agreed."

Kali's tribe had assessed the dangerous task of moving a bridge as thoroughly as possible and adjusted as unforeseen problems arose. They'd created a think tank and worked together, keeping panic to a minimum. They'd even recorded the whole process should another bridge ever need to be built. Their ability to assess and minimize risk had led to their success. He filled out the worksheet T-chart and created a second one on the back.

What Makes Mitigating Risk Fail	What Makes Handling Risk Succeed
• Punishing mistakes	• Good planning
• Fear of failure	• Good decision making
• Criticism	• Accountability
• Unclear goals and procedures	• Utilizing mistakes as learning opportunities
• Perfectionism and over-analysis	• Documenting successful procedures

Why I'm not handling risk correctly	How I need to handle risk
• I get angry or fire people for making mistakes	• Change mindset towards mistakes and failure
• I don't listen when people see a problem	• Collaborate instead of criticize
• No one knows what the real goal is	• Establish clear goals
• Perfectionism is stalling progress	• Nix my micromanaging
• My fear of failure is making us fail	• Bring fear to heel
	• Train employees in planning and decision making

Derek jotted down several more things he wanted to address as soon as he could talk to Catherine and his team. He had to create a work environment that felt like a safe place for them to learn and grow. This was the end of fearing every mistake or failure was the end of their careers. Somehow, he'd forgotten this as soon as work grew more stressful. Remembering it filled him with hope and newfound energy. Tomorrow was going to be a great day.

The final trial/principle on the list was *success*. Derek made some notes on it and sat back in his chair. "I must admit that at first I was skeptical when Kali let his tribe members have a say on how to build the bridge. I'm the project manager because I'm the detail person. I earned the right to tell people what to do and how to do it, but the truth is, you can see a rounder picture with more eyes on the task at hand. On top of that, it makes people more committed to the overall goal. When Kali told everyone they were staying in the village when the storm hit, it's clear to me now that they felt controlled and trapped in someone else's decision. No one was happy and Kali had to force animals to listen. But, when he gave his tribe a chance to offer input on how to build the bridge, they were so eager to help and they ended up doing a great job. Their ideas added to the goal and they were happy. And Kali was happy because they were happy."

Derek tackled the Success part of the worksheet.

Why People/Teams Don't Create Success	Why People/Teams Create Success
• Lack of commitment to a clear goal • Poor directions/ procedures • Ambivalent employees • Confusion	• Clear goals and directions • Clear directions and procedures • Engaged and satisfied employees • Acknowledgement and recognition of their success

"I've forgotten about everyone's happiness—even my own. I've been so focused on deadlines and completing projects that when the work wasn't getting done on time, I wasn't asking what was wrong or if anyone needed help. I was getting angry and reprimanding them. That changes tomorrow, too. I need to be part of the solution, instead of the problem."

"I wholeheartedly believe you will be." Martha gave him one more kiss and headed off to their bedroom to read.

Normally, Derek would do the same but he felt too wired. He made one last T-chart on the back of the worksheet.

Why the team is failing	How to help us succeed
• Me in so many ways	• Teach both myself and my employees to become TIGERS
	• Focus more on quality work and the satisfaction of my people doing the quality work

At first, he thought he had more to say, but the two bullet points summarized everything. Ideas bounced around in his head and he found himself jotting down pages and pages of ideas in his notebook. There were things he wanted to change, questions he wanted to ask specific people, and so on. He didn't stop until Martha came down hours later, asking if he was okay.

He was more than okay. For the first time in a long time, he couldn't wait to get to work the next day. However, he made himself brush his teeth and head to bed. Despite wanting to sleep, his mind kept working into the small hours of the morning before the exhaustion finally hit.

Derek Alexander headed into work the next morning with a fresh suit, straight tie, shiny shoes and a children's book. He also went in with two things he hadn't brought with him in a long time: a genuine smile and a good plan. He was going to have an office full of TIGERS, and he was determined to be the best leader he could be.

The Beginning!

Also by Dianne Crampton

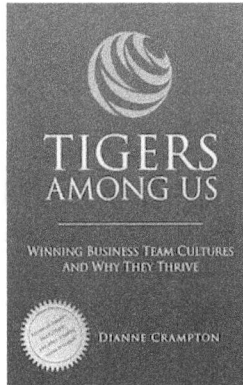

TIGERS Among Us – Winning Business Team Cultures and Why They Thrive (Three Creeks, 2010)

TIGERS Among Us provides business owners and managers a path for building an authentic, team-based work culture. Based on the TIGERS model of collaborative principles – trust, interdependence, genuineness, empathy, risk and success – this book describes breakthrough practices for instilling collaboration in the workplace. It shows how the creation of an authentic team culture in your workplace will result in optimum productivity for your business, and personal and professional fulfillment for your employees.

It is far more than simply a business model. This book shows what an authentic team-based culture actually looks like in the workplace – how it functions and why it works. Here you will find detailed descriptions of four diverse, winning businesses – Zappos.com, Tribe Inc., 4Refuel and Dos Gringos – and learn the steps their leaders took to build successful team cultures. They did it, and so can you. Take this book home with you today.

Multiple book discounts for leadership teams, consultants, coaches and start ups at http://www.TigersAmongUs.com

Forming TIGERS®-Hearted Teams (Pfeiffer and imprint of John Wiles and Sons, 2010)

> Collaborative work cultures that pay attention to group norm behaviors such as trust, interdependence, genuineness, empathy, risk and success in the workplace are important to today's economy. In February 2007, the U.S. Small Business Administration reported that small businesses, comprised of five hundred or fewer employees, are the largest employment segment in the country. They are the backbone of the U.S. economy. Yet many of these companies, some strikingly fast-growing, find themselves struggling with issues such as attracting talented team members and sustaining growth. A survey conducted by TIGERS Success Series in 2007 concluded that the number one reason talented employees leave companies is because they will not accept a poor company culture or attitudes that violate values, such as trust, when other work opportunities are present. TIGERS is a leadership model that provides a foundation for success.

The 2010 Pfeiffer Annual Consulting
The Leader in Resources for Training and HR Professionals for the Past Four Decades.

The 2010 Pfeiffer Consulting Annual is a ready-made toolkit of ideas, methods, techniques, and models that assist and support your work as an internal or external organizational consultant. The Annual addresses the broad range of topics that are of most interest to professionals in the field. The materials provide highly accessible means of interacting with a diverse variety of systems and processes – from collaborative work systems and executive coaching to strategic planning and organizational development.

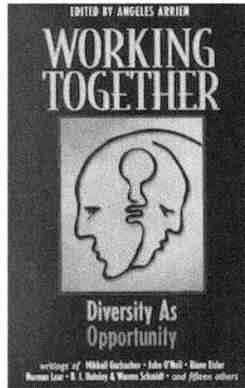

Working Together – Producing Synergy by Honoring Diversity
(Berrett Koehler 2003)

Interdependence: A Matter of Practical Diversity

Finally, a book that looks at diversity as an advantage to be utilized and not a problem to be solved.

Based on an incredible array of contributing authors, this groundbreaking anthology examines the subject of diversity from a holistic perspective – as a context for creating synergy in our projects, our organizations and our lives.

This book is about honoring diversity for the incredible rich resource it truly represents, and not coping with it or dealing with it as a burden of the times. Learning to honor diversity, recognizing its value, and working with the multitude of viewpoints it brings with it are all part of a larger evolutionary shift. This shift is one of the most profound shifts ever experienced by human beings and will be looked back upon as a major historic leap in the growing consciousness of our planet.

ABOUT THE AUTHOR

Dianne Crampton is one of North America's leading experts on corporate team culture and is a sought-after Culture Change and Workforce Development Consultant, Workforce Behavior Improvement Coach, Speaker and Author.

Crampton is the founder and president of TIGERS® Success Series, Inc., a trademarked team development process that illuminates 6 Principles that measurably improve workforce behavior and work culture. The TIGERS 6 Principles™ are trust, interdependence, genuineness, empathy, risk and success.

In her many years of comprehensive research, Crampton discovered that these six principles are necessary for building ethical, quality-focused, productive, motivated and successful groups of people. Her company URL is http://www.corevalues. com .

For more than 20 years, Crampton has used TIGERS Success Series to work with motivated leaders and their employees. She helps committed leaders build work cultures where cooperation among employees and collaboration between departments drive growth and revenue.

Through consultation, the TIGERS Workforce Behavioral Profile™—a 360 team behavior assessment—and a comprehensive system of team improvement activities and online training and development, Crampton teaches companies of all sizes how to evolve from being good to exceptional.

STAY CONNECTED

Why struggle in the jungle when you don't have to?

Provide Becoming TIGERS – Leading Your Team to Success for Your Team At Healthy Discounts.
Volume discounts available through Three Creeks Publishing at www.BecomingTIGERS.com.

Consider TIGERS 6 Principles Micro-Training for All Your Leaders.
Micro-training is for teams and leaders available at www.corevalues.com.

Determine the Quality of Trust, Interdependence, Genuineness, Empathy, Risk and Success In Your Organization.
Learn about the TIGERS Workforce Behavioral Profile™ at www.TigersSuccessSeries.com.

Speaking and Presentations – Invite Dianne Crampton to Speak at Your Next Conference, Meeting, or Business Event.
Contact our public relations team at prghuru@corevalues.com.

Give us a review. We love it when you do!

www.ingramcontent.com/pod-product-compliance
Lightning Source LLC
Chambersburg PA
CBHW071915200326
41519CB00016B/4623